BISTRO

RYLAND
PETERS
& SMALL

LONDON NEW YORK

BISTRO

French country recipes for home cooks

Laura Washburn

Photography by Martin Brigdale

First published in Great Britain in 2003

This paperback edition published in 2008
by Ryland Peters & Small
20–21 Jockey's Fields
London WC1R 4BW
www.rylandpeters.com

10 9 8 7 6 5 4 3 2 1

ISBN 978 1 84597 693 4

A catalogue record for this book is available
from the British Library.

Printed and bound in China

Senior Designer Steve Painter
Commissioning Editor Elsa Petersen-Schepelern
Production Meryl Silbert
Art Director Gabriella Le Grazie
Publishing Director Alison Starling

Food Stylist Linda Tubby
Stylist Helen Trent
Indexer Hilary Bird

Dedication

For Mom and John

Acknowledgements

Thank you to all who helped with the children,
especially Melissa Glase and Rachel Donovan,
but also Gail Ezra, Denise Clare and Linda
Daniels. Thanks also to the Phillips family; Maha,
Mike, Lawrence and Martha, who graciously gave
up many a Sunday to help with the eating and
critiquing. Wine and food matching advice came
from the experts at Apogée, Patrice and Erika
Marcoue, Le Puiset, France www.vinsapogee.com.
Thank you, Martin Brigdale, Linda Tubby and
Helen Trent for making it look so beautiful, and
thanks to Steve Painter for enthusiasm and
helpful input, as well as great design. Thanks,
Ananda. And thanks, thanks, thanks to Julian,
Clara and especially Jim.

Notes

•All spoon measurements are level unless
otherwise stated.

•Ingredients in this book are available from
larger supermarkets, specialist greengrocers and
delicatessens. See page 142 for mail order
sources.

•Ovens should be preheated to the specified
temperature. Recipes in this book were tested
using a conventional oven. If using a fan oven,
cooking times should be changed according to
the manufacturer's instructions.

•For all recipes requiring dough or batter, liquid
measurements are given as a guide. Always add
liquid gradually to achieve the desired consistency,
rather than adding it all at once. Use your eyes
and your sense of touch to achieve the best
results. If you don't use the flour specified in a
recipe, the result may be affected.

contents

Suggestion
Potjevlesch
12€

LEFFE
BRUNE
PRESSION 25cl

Suggestion
Moules
Marinière
12

Croustillant aux Vieux Lille
Terrine du Nord
* Carbonnade à la Bière
* Lapin à la Flamande
* Andouillette de St Géry

* Tarte à la Chicorée
* Glace à la Chicorée
* Assiette de fromage
(Vieux lille maroilles)

SUGGESTIONS
* Salade de Crottin 6,3
* Fricassé d'Anguille
en Matelote 12,50
* Onglet de veau
à l'échalote 11€
* Glace Pain d'épice
et sa tulipe 5

LA VOUTE
RESTAURANT

bistro is a way of life

People disagree about the origins of the word 'bistro'. Some say it was introduced by the Russians after the invasion of Paris in 1814, as they shouted *'bystro!'* (meaning 'quickly!') at waiters in busy cafés. Some argue that it evolved from the Parisian slang of the time, and others trace the term to a northern dialect. But wherever the word began, the bistro experience has not strayed too far from its roots.

Restaurants and cafés sprang up all over France during the 19th century, primarily in Paris, but these upscale eating establishments were destined for the bourgeoisie. Bistros began at about the same time and the difference was in the clientele, the locality and the atmosphere of the place. They were neighbourhood watering-holes, a sanctuary for the locals, a comforting, relaxed place for people to gather and socialize. Initially, bistros were as much about drinking as eating. Simple country wines were poured from carafes into chunky water glasses while the regulars debated the political topics of the day. But this sort of activity requires sustenance and, gradually, bistros became like extensions of the home kitchen. So while 'chefs' prepared elegant meals in the *grands restaurants*, cooks prepared modest food for the ordinary folk in local bistros.

Nowadays, the distinctions are blurred, and the terms 'bistro' and 'restaurant' are used almost interchangeably. Despite this, there does seem to be an implicit understanding that bistro is synonymous with simplicity. The reason is that bistro food is traditional, with roots in the regional specialities of France. For the most part, bistro menus often mimic the kind of meals prepared in homes. This is why authentic bistro fare is the essence of French cuisine. It is honest, fresh and satisfying food prepared by cooks, not celebrity chefs. It uses local ingredients and seasonal produce. It is not expensive, it is not complicated and it never goes out of fashion. Bistro food is real food, for real people.

There is nothing new about bistro. The recipes in this book are simply up-to-date versions of good, old-fashioned food. And despite all the conveniences of modern life, time is still short, so ingredients are basic, preparations are simple and, for the health-conscious, butter and cream have been kept to a minimum. Suggestions for French regional wines to accompany many of the dishes have been provided because the best thing to drink with French food is French wine. It's also part of the fun. Bistro food started in home kitchens, so there is no need for fancy equipment or great technical prowess. Better still, bistro is about making the most of ingredients; it's about value for money and it's about cooking with leftovers.

The stresses of life were surely different in the days when bistros began, but our need to escape, to relax and to restore ourselves remains the same. Bistro food is like a trusted friend. It is reliable, it is comfortable, it is easy. It is what you want to come home to after a hard day's work. So the trends may come, and the trends will surely go, but one thing that will remain constant is our appetite for authentic flavours and satisfying meals, which is why bistro cooking has enduring appeal.

But bistro is more than just cuisine. It's a way of life. It's about taking the time to savour a meal and enjoy the company of family and friends. Bistro cooking is about bringing the pot straight to the table, dipping chunks of crusty baguette in a rich, simmered sauce and washing it all down with French country wine. Bistro cuisine represents the best that France has to offer and the next best thing to being there (in France!) is to bring a bit of bistro to your own home. *Bon appétit!*

starters

This recipe is my version of a well-loved staple of Provençal cuisine. Purists will tell you that only Parisians add carrots and that aged Gouda is imperative. The reason, according to one story, is that this soup was invented by Italian workers building the railway in the hills above Nice, who used the Dutch cheese because there was a lot of it in transit at the port. A variation is to add skinned, deseeded and chopped tomatoes to the pistou.

soupe au pistou

3 tablespoons extra virgin olive oil

1 onion, chopped

1 small fennel bulb, quartered, cored and chopped

2 courgettes, chopped

200 g new potatoes, chopped

2 tomatoes, skinned, deseeded and chopped

2 litres vegetable or chicken stock*

a sprig of thyme

400 g canned cannellini beans, drained

400 g canned red kidney beans, drained

150 g green beans, cut into 3 cm pieces

50 g spaghetti, broken into pieces

150 g finely grated cheese (aged Gouda or Parmesan)

coarse sea salt and freshly ground black pepper

Pistou

6 garlic cloves

a small bunch of basil, leaves only

6 tablespoons extra virgin olive oil

Serves 4–6

Heat the oil in a large saucepan or casserole dish. Add the onion, fennel and courgettes and cook over medium heat until browned, about 10 minutes. Add the potatoes, tomatoes, stock and thyme. Bring to the boil, then cover and simmer gently for 15 minutes.

Add the canned cannellini and kidney beans and simmer, covered, for 15 minutes more. Taste and adjust the seasoning with salt and pepper. Add the green beans and the spaghetti and cook until the pasta is tender, about 10 minutes more. Cover and let stand. Ideally, the soup should rest for at least a few hours before serving, or make one day in advance and refrigerate. (Do not make the pistou until you are ready to serve; it is best fresh, and the basil and garlic should not be cooked.)

To make the pistou, put the garlic, basil and oil in a small food processor and blend until well chopped. You can also make it using a mortar and pestle, starting with the garlic and finishing with the oil, added gradually. It is more authentic, but I've never been very good at this method.

To serve, heat the soup and pass round the pistou and cheese, to be stirred in to taste. The soup can also be served at room temperature.

*Note Unless your stock is homemade, it probably contains salt, so season judiciously and taste the soup often as it cooks.

A classic case of less is more. This soup is soothing and restorative, and deliciously delicate, despite its rustic origins. Homemade salt pork makes all the difference to the taste and is very simple to make. You will have to sacrifice some refrigerator space for three days, which is the only complication, but you will be well rewarded. Your butcher should be able to supply the salt.

cabbage soup
soupe au chou

750 g pork belly, sliced

100 g pickling salt

1 onion, studded with a clove

1 fresh bay leaf

1 cabbage

1 inner celery stalk with leaves, cut into chunks

7 carrots, cut into chunks

4 turnips, cut into chunks

1 tablespoon unsalted butter, plus more for serving

750 g small new potatoes, peeled

coarse sea salt

Serves 4–6

Three days before you plan to serve the soup, put the pork belly slices in a shallow ceramic or glass dish and add water to cover. Add the salt and stir until dissolved. Cover and refrigerate for 3 days, turning occasionally. Alternatively, have the butcher salt the pork belly for you.

The day of serving, remove the pork belly from its brine and rinse. Put the pork and onion in a large saucepan with 3 litres water. Bring to the boil and skim off any foam that rises to the surface, then reduce the heat, cover and let simmer.

Meanwhile, bring another saucepan of water to the boil with a bay leaf. When it boils, add the cabbage and blanch for 5 minutes. Remove the cabbage and drain. When cool enough to handle, slice the cabbage.

Add the sliced cabbage, celery, carrots, turnips and butter to the pork. Taste for seasoning; it may not even need salt because of the salt pork. Return to the boil, then lower the heat, cover and simmer for about 30 minutes. Taste for seasoning again.

Add the potatoes and cook until they are tender, 20–25 minutes more. To serve, remove the pork belly and cut into bite-sized pieces. Trim off any rind and discard any bones. Return the pork pieces to the soup and serve hot, with a spoonful of butter in each bowl and thick slices of country bread.

Note If you don't have time to salt the pork yourself, buy a smoked pork knuckle from the butcher and proceed as in the main recipe.

An old-fashioned nourishing soup, full of healthy green things. If you do not have sorrel growing in your garden (or available in your supermarket), it can be omitted.

kitchen garden soup
soupe du potager

1 fresh bay leaf

1 small cabbage, quartered

60 g unsalted butter

2 leeks, halved and sliced

1 onion, chopped

2 teaspoons salt

250 g new potatoes, chopped

a handful of flat leaf parsley, chopped

250 g fresh shelled peas

1 Little Gem lettuce, quartered and sliced thinly

a bunch of sorrel, sliced

unsalted butter and/or crème fraîche, to serve (optional)

sea salt and freshly ground black pepper

Serves 4–6

Put the bay leaf in a large saucepan of water and bring to the boil. Add the cabbage quarters and blanch for 3 minutes. Drain the cabbage, pat dry and slice it thinly.

Heat the butter in a large saucepan. Add the cabbage, leeks, onion and 2 teaspoons salt and cook until softened, 5–10 minutes. Add the potatoes, parsley and 2 litres water. Add salt and pepper to taste and simmer gently for 40 minutes.

Stir in the peas, lettuce and sorrel and cook for 10 minutes more. Taste for seasoning. Ladle into bowls, add 1 tablespoon of butter and/or crème fraîche, if using, to each and serve.

It is difficult to make true bouillabaisse outside France because so many of the fish used are found only in the Mediterranean. But here's a very good vegetable-only alternative, with all the same flavours, including the best part – the chilli-spiked rouille sauce. Traditional versions include a poached egg, which I have omitted.

vegetable bouillabaisse
bouillabaisse borgne

4 tablespoons extra virgin olive oil

2 leeks, white part only, halved lengthways, then sliced crossways

1 large onion, coarsely chopped

1 fennel bulb, halved, cored and chopped

3 garlic cloves, crushed

3 large ripe tomatoes, skinned, deseeded and chopped

5 medium new potatoes, cubed

1 teaspoon salt

2 litres vegetable stock or water*

1 fresh bay leaf

a sprig of thyme

a strip of peel from 1 unwaxed orange

1 teaspoon good-quality saffron strands

1 baguette loaf, sliced, for croutons

100 g freshly grated Gruyère cheese

coarse sea salt and freshly ground black pepper

a handful of chopped flat leaf parsley, to serve

Rouille

3 garlic cloves, very finely chopped

1–2 red chillies, deseeded and very finely chopped

1 egg yolk, at room temperature

about 300 ml extra virgin olive oil

fine sea salt and freshly ground black pepper

a baking tray

Serves 4–6

Heat the oil in a large saucepan. Add the leeks, onions and fennel and cook until just beginning to brown, about 10 minutes. Stir in the garlic, tomatoes, potatoes and 1 teaspoon salt and cook for 1 minute. Add the stock or water, the bay leaf, thyme, orange peel and saffron and stir. Bring to the boil, reduce the heat and simmer gently until the potatoes are tender, about 40 minutes. Add salt and pepper to taste, cover and let stand for at least 1 hour, or cool and refrigerate overnight.

Before you serve, make the croutons. Arrange the baguette slices in a single layer on a baking tray. Bake in a preheated oven at 180°C (350°F) Gas 4 until golden, about 5–8 minutes. Set aside.

To make the rouille, put the garlic, chillies and egg yolk in a small, deep bowl. Beat well. Add the oil bit by bit and beating vigorously, until the mixture is thick like mayonnaise. Add fine salt and pepper to taste.

To serve, warm the soup if necessary. Put 2–3 croutons in each soup plate, sprinkle with the grated cheese and ladle in the soup. Sprinkle with chopped parsley and serve with the rouille, to be stirred in according to taste.

*Note Unless your stock is homemade, it probably contains salt, so season judiciously and taste the soup often as it cooks.

Although this soup is synonymous with bistro eating, it is also associated with another tradition. At French weddings, especially in the countryside, it was often served in the early hours of the morning, as a restorative after a long night of celebrating. This recipe is a simplified version, the sort of thing that's ideal when it's chilly outside, people are hungry inside and there's not much more than a few onions lurking about.

french onion soup
soupe gratinée à l'oignon

50 g unsalted butter

1 tablespoon extra virgin olive oil

3 large onions, about 1.3 kg, thinly sliced

2 garlic cloves, crushed

1 tablespoon plain flour

1 litre beef or chicken stock

600 ml dry white wine

1 fresh bay leaf

2 sprigs of thyme

1 baguette, or other white bread, sliced

about 180 g freshly grated Gruyère cheese

coarse sea salt and freshly ground black pepper

a baking tray

Serves 4–6

Put the butter and oil in a large saucepan and melt over medium heat. Add the onions and cook over low heat until soft, 15–20 minutes.

Add the garlic and flour and cook, stirring for about 1 minute. Add the stock, wine, bay leaf and thyme. Season with salt and pepper and bring to the boil. Boil for 1 minute, then lower the heat and simmer very gently for 20 minutes. Taste and adjust the seasoning with salt and pepper. At this point, the soup will be cooked, but standing time will improve the flavour – at least 30 minutes.

Before serving, preheat the grill. Put the baguette slices on a baking tray and brown under the grill until lightly toasted. Set aside.

To serve, ladle the soup into ovenproof bowls and top with a few toasted baguette rounds. Sprinkle grated cheese over the top and cook under the grill until browned and bubbling. Serve immediately.

France has many fish soups but only this one includes hot chillies. Another plus is that it can be made successfully without hard-to-come-by Mediterranean fish and, if you use good-quality fresh fish stock, it's very quick to make. The bones and prawn shells add flavour, as well as making it a bit messy, but this is fishermen's fare, so roll up your sleeves and enjoy.

basque fish soup

ttoro

2 tablespoons extra virgin olive oil

1 red pepper, halved, deseeded and sliced

1 onion, halved and sliced

3 garlic cloves, crushed

1 green chilli, deseeded and chopped

¼ teaspoon best-quality hot paprika

a sprig of thyme

225 g canned chopped peeled tomatoes

1.5 litres fresh fish stock

250 g monkfish fillet, cut into bite-sized pieces

500 g hake or cod steaks

250 g unpeeled prawn tails

250 ml dry white wine

500 g fresh mussels*

a handful of flat leaf parsley, chopped

Croutons

1 baguette, sliced

2 garlic cloves, peeled

Serves 4–6

Heat the oil in a stockpot. Add the pepper and onion and cook until browned, about 5 minutes. Stir in the garlic, chilli, paprika, thyme and tomatoes and cook for 5 minutes more.

Add the fish stock, monkfish, hake and prawns. Bring to the boil, skim off the foam and simmer gently until the fish is cooked through, 10–15 minutes.

Meanwhile, to make the croutons, arrange the baguette slices in a single layer on a baking tray. Bake in a preheated oven at 180°C (350°F) Gas 4 until golden, 5–8 minutes. Let cool slightly, then rub with garlic cloves and set aside.

Pour the wine into a large saucepan with a lid and bring to the boil for 1 minute, then remove from the heat. Add the prepared mussels to the wine, cover and steam over high heat just until opened, 2–3 minutes. Remove the mussels from their shells, discarding any that do not open.

Add the mussels and cooking liquid to the soup and stir well. Sprinkle with parsley and serve immediately, with the garlic croutons.

*Note To prepare mussels, start 15 minutes before you are ready to use. Rinse them in cold water and tap any open ones against the work surface. If they don't close, discard them. Scrub the others with a stiff brush and scrape off any barnacles. Pull off and discard the wiry beards.

Unlike most dishes cooked with cheese, this is very light and elegant, perfect to serve before a rich stew. It is also very moreish and you could be tempted to make a meal of it with a simple green salad. Alternatively, you could make individual tarts for a picnic, buffet or dinner party. Serve with a white wine from the Loire.

goats' cheese tart
tarte au chèvre

200 g plain flour, plus extra for rolling
100 g cold unsalted butter, cut into pieces
a pinch of salt
3–4 tablespoons cold water

Goats' cheese filling
3 eggs
200 ml crème fraîche
3 Crottin de Chavignol goats' cheeses, about 50–75 g each
50 g finely grated Gruyère cheese
a small bunch of chives
fine sea salt

baking parchment and beans or baking weights
a loose-based tart tin, 27 cm diameter

Serves 4–6

To make the pastry, put the flour, butter and salt in a food processor and, using the pulse button, process until the butter is broken down (about 5–10 pulses). Add 3 tablespoons cold water and pulse just until the mixture forms coarse crumbs; add 1 more tablespoon if necessary, but do not do more than 10 pulses.

Transfer the pastry to a sheet of baking parchment, form into a ball and flatten to a disc. Wrap in the parchment paper and refrigerate for 30–60 minutes.

Roll out the pastry on a floured work surface to a disc slightly larger than the tart tin. Carefully transfer the pastry to the tin, patching any holes as you go and pressing gently into the sides. To trim the edges, roll a rolling pin over the top, using the edge of the tin as a cutting surface and let the excess fall away. Tidy up the edges and refrigerate until firm, about 30–60 minutes.

Prick the pastry all over, line with the baking parchment and fill with beans or baking weights. Bake in a preheated oven at 200°C (400°F) Gas 6 for 15 minutes, then remove the paper and weights and bake until just golden, about 10–15 minutes more. Let the tart shell cool slightly before filling.

To make the filling, put the eggs, crème fraîche and a large pinch of salt in a bowl and whisk well. Slice each goats' cheese into 3 rounds and arrange in the tart shell. Pour in the egg mixture and sprinkle with the Gruyère. Snip the chives with kitchen scissors and sprinkle over the top.

Bake in the preheated oven at 200°C (400°F) Gas 6 for 20–30 minutes or until browned. Serve warm.

Green salads do not appear as often on French menus as a starter or side dish as they do in other countries, though they are still served in very traditional bistros. Home is the main place for eating salads, and they're eaten daily, usually after the main course and either before or with the cheese. Raw garlic is not always included, but the vinaigrette method is classic, the way I was taught to make it when I first moved to France, and the way I've made it ever since.

mixed greens with garlic vinaigrette
salade verte, vinaigrette à l'ail

2 tablespoons wine vinegar

½ teaspoon fine sea salt

1 teaspoon Dijon mustard

6 tablespoons extra virgin olive oil

2 garlic cloves, crushed

freshly ground pepper

250 g tender, mixed salad greens, washed and dried

a handful of flat leaf parsley, coarsely chopped

a small bunch of chives, snipped with kitchen scissors

Serves 4

Put the vinegar in the salad bowl. Using a fork or a small whisk, stir in the salt until almost dissolved. You may have to tilt the bowl so the vinegar is deep enough to have something to stir around. Stir in the mustard until completely blended. Add the oil, a tablespoon at a time, beating well between each addition, until emulsified. Mix in the garlic and pepper to taste.

If you like a powerful garlic punch, tear the lettuce in smallish pieces, add to the bowl with the parsley and chives, then toss. Serve immediately. I prefer to let the garlic sit in the dressing for at least 30 minutes to mellow it a bit. In any case, do not add the lettuce until you are ready to serve or it will go soggy.

Anchoïade is a Provençal anchovy sauce/dip, which is spread thickly on grilled bread slices, or served with raw vegetables as a starter. Here it becomes a dressing for what will hopefully be very ripe, flavourful tomatoes. If these are not available, use boiled baby new potatoes instead and toss while the potatoes are still warm. Serve with a chilled Provençal rosé and lots of crusty bread.

750 g ripe vine tomatoes

I large shallot, or I small red onion, thinly sliced

coarse sea salt and freshly ground black pepper

Anchovy vinaigrette

I garlic clove

½ teaspoon Dijon mustard

2 tablespoons white wine vinegar

6 anchovy fillets, packed in oil

8 tablespoons extra virgin olive oil

a small handful of basil leaves

freshly ground black pepper

To serve

a handful of flat leaf parsley, finely chopped

a few basil leaves, torn

Serves 4

tomato salad with anchovy vinaigrette
salade de tomates, vinaigrette à l'anchoïade

To make the vinaigrette, put the garlic, mustard, vinegar and anchovies in a small food processor and blend well. Add the oil, I tablespoon at a time, then blend in the basil. Season with pepper and set aside.

Cut the tomatoes into quarters or eighths, depending on their size. Arrange on a plate and sprinkle with the shallot. Season lightly with salt, then spoon the dressing over the top. Sprinkle with the parsley, basil and freshly ground black pepper, and serve at room temperature.

chicory salad with roquefort, celery and walnuts

salade d'endives aux roquefort, céleri et noix

4–5 heads of chicory, about 600 g, halved, cored and thinly sliced

2 celery stalks, thinly sliced, plus a few leaves, torn

75 g Roquefort cheese, crumbled

50 g shelled walnuts, chopped

a handful of flat leaf parsley, finely chopped

1 baguette, sliced, to serve

Walnut vinaigrette

2 tablespoons wine vinegar

1 teaspoon fine sea salt

1 teaspoon Dijon mustard

7 tablespoons sunflower oil (see method)

1 tablespoon walnut oil (optional)

freshly ground pepper

Serves 4

Mine is a family of serial salad eaters, but I'd never heard of chicory until moving to France. In those days, it was still a fairly bitter thing, available only in winter and an acquired taste, but it has come a long way. Developed unintentionally by a gardener at the Brussels botanical gardens in the middle of the nineteenth century, chicory is now cultivated for a good part of the year, and modern varieties have none of the bitterness of their ancestors. When buying, choose very pale chicory with only a hint of green; they grow in the dark, so colour on the leaves is a sign that they have been exposed to the light and are not as fresh. Also, big is not necessarily better; 20 cm is the maximum length for best taste.

To prepare the vinaigrette, put the vinegar in the salad bowl. Using a fork or a small whisk, stir in the salt until almost dissolved. You may have to tilt the bowl so the vinegar is deep enough to have something to stir. Mix in the mustard until completely blended. Add the oil, a tablespoon at a time, beating well between each addition, until emulsified. If you're using the walnut oil, use one less tablespoon of sunflower oil. Stir in pepper to taste.

Just before you're ready to serve the salad, add the chicory, celery, Roquefort, walnuts and parsley and toss well. Serve immediately, with a basket of sliced baguette.

Before school holidays imposed August-only restrictions on our travel, we always went to Cassis in September. We loved to picnic in the middle *calanque* – swimming, sunning and, of course, eating. For the occasion, I would buy this salad from a tiny butcher's shop in the back lanes. It was made by an Algerian, which explains the cumin and makes all the difference.

chickpea salad
salade de pois chiches

250 g dried chickpeas

1 fresh bay leaf

2 red peppers, halved, deseeded and sliced

2 tablespoons extra virgin olive oil

1 teaspoon herbes de provence

1 large shallot, chopped

a large handful of flat leaf parsley, chopped

coarse sea salt and freshly ground black pepper

Vinaigrette

2 teaspoons cumin seeds

3 tablespoons wine vinegar

1 teaspoon fine sea salt

10 tablespoons extra virgin olive oil

freshly ground black pepper

Serves 4–6

One day before serving, soak the chickpeas in cold water to cover, and put in the refrigerator. Drain the chickpeas. Transfer to a saucepan and cover with cold water. Add the bay leaf and bring to the boil. When the water boils, lower the heat, cover and simmer until tender, about 2 hours. Check occasionally and add more water if necessary. Add 1 teaspoon coarse sea salt 30 minutes before the end of cooking time.

Meanwhile, put the peppers in a small baking dish, toss with the oil, herbs and 1 teaspoon salt. Roast in a preheated oven at 220°C (425°F) Gas 7 until beginning to char, 20–25 minutes. Remove from the oven. When cool, cut into dice and set aside.

To make the vinaigrette, dry-fry the cumin seeds in a hot frying pan until they begin to pop and you can smell their aroma. Immediately crush them to a powder with a mortar and pestle.

Put the vinegar in a small bowl. Using a fork or a small whisk, stir in the fine sea salt until almost dissolved. You may have to tilt the bowl so the vinegar is deep enough to have something to stir. Add the oil, a tablespoon at a time, whisking well between each addition, until emulsified. Mix in the cumin and pepper to taste.

When the chickpeas are cooked, drain thoroughly and transfer to a serving bowl; a wide, shallow one is best, to ensure a maximum of dressing comes into contact with the chickpeas. Add the vinaigrette, red pepper and shallot. Toss well and add salt and pepper to taste. Add the parsley, toss again and serve warm or at room temperature.

Crudités are a classic starter, especially in Parisian cafés and bistros, and they are a favourite of mine. The combination of vegetables given is fairly representative, but it does vary. Canned corn and tuna are common, as are hard-boiled eggs. You could quite easily make a meal of this by increasing the quantities or adding other ingredients to make it more elegant and contemporary. Try blanched asparagus tips, sliced cherry tomatoes, peeled blanched broad beans or wafer-thin red onion slices.

crudités

2 tablespoons wine vinegar

¼ red cabbage, thinly sliced

250 g baby new potatoes

125 g baby green beans, topped and tailed

3 medium carrots, grated

1 tablespoon freshly squeezed lemon juice

3 cooked beetroot

175 g cucumber

a handful of flat leaf parsley, finely chopped

fine sea salt

1 baguette, sliced, to serve

Vinaigrette

3 tablespoons wine vinegar

1 teaspoon fine sea salt

2 teaspoons Dijon mustard

11 tablespoons sunflower oil

freshly ground black pepper

Serves 4

To make the vinaigrette, put the vinegar in a bowl. Using a fork or a small whisk, stir in the salt until almost dissolved. You may have to tilt the bowl so the vinegar is deep enough to have something to stir. Mix in the mustard until completely blended. Add the oil, 1 tablespoon at a time, whisking well between each addition, until emulsified. Add pepper to taste. Set aside.

Heat the vinegar in a wok. As soon as it boils, remove from the heat, add the red cabbage and toss well. Salt lightly and set aside until the cabbage turns an even deep, fuchsia colour.

Meanwhile, put the potatoes in a saucepan with cold water to cover. Bring to the boil, add salt and cook until tender, about 15 minutes. Drain, peel and slice thinly.

Bring another saucepan of water to the boil, add salt, then the beans. Cook until just tender, 3–5 minutes. Drain and set aside.

Put the carrots, lemon juice and a pinch of salt in a bowl and toss well; set aside. Cut the beetroot in quarters lengthways, then slice thinly to get small triangular pieces. Peel the cucumber (if you like), cut it in quarters lengthways and slice.

Arrange small mounds of each ingredient on plates, alternating colours. Add a few spoonfuls of vinaigrette to each one and sprinkle with parsley. Serve with a basket of sliced baguette.

Light lovely leeks in a lively herb-studded sauce. Serve these at the start of a substantial spread, to allow room for expansion, or as part of a light lunch, with the Goats' Cheese Tart on page 22. If you can't find sorrel, it will be a shame, but the recipe works without, so don't feel obliged to replace it with anything.

baby leeks
with herb vinaigrette
poireaux, vinaigrette aux herbes

750 g baby leeks

60 ml wine vinegar

1 teaspoon Dijon mustard

1 teaspoon fine sea salt

250 ml sunflower oil

a small handful of flat leaf parsley

a small handful of watercress

a small handful of tarragon

3 sorrel leaves

freshly ground black pepper

2 shallots, thinly sliced

a small bunch of chives, scissor-snipped

Serves 4

Put the leeks in the top of a steamer and cook until tender, about 7–10 minutes. Remove and set aside to drain.

To make the vinaigrette, put the vinegar, mustard and salt in a small food processor and blend well. Add about 75 ml of the oil and blend for a few seconds. Continue adding the oil, bit by bit, and blending until the vinaigrette is emulsified. Add the parsley, watercress, tarragon and sorrel and pulse again to chop. Add pepper to taste. (Alternatively, see page 25 for the hand-mixing method, and you'll have to chop all the herbs finely.)

If the leeks are still too wet, pat dry with kitchen paper. Arrange the leeks in a serving dish, spoon the vinaigrette over the top and sprinkle with shallot slices and chives. Serve with any remaining vinaigrette on the side.

mackerel pâté

rillettes de maquereaux

2 mackerel, about 400 g each, well cleaned, with heads on

1 onion, sliced

40 g unsalted butter, cut into pieces and melted or softened

a large handful of flat leaf parsley

a few sprigs of tarragon, leaves stripped

freshly squeezed juice of 1 lemon

a dash of Tabasco

coarse sea salt and freshly ground black pepper

Court bouillon

1 carrot, sliced

1 onion, sliced

1 organic lemon, sliced

1 sprig of thyme

1 fresh bay leaf

a few black peppercorns

1 clove

1 bottle dry white wine

2 teaspoons salt

To serve

toast or baguette

lemon wedges

Serves 6–8

Rillettes, a coarse but spreadable pâté, is normally made from pork or goose. This is a lighter version, made from mackerel poached in white wine, giving it a pleasant, almost pickled taste. Serve this straight from the bowl, passing it around the table at the start of an informal gathering, or spread it on crackers and serve with drinks. There's no point making this in small batches – but it freezes well, in case this is more than you need, or if you have leftovers.

One day before serving, put all the court bouillon ingredients in a saucepan. Bring to the boil over high heat, boil for 1 minute, then cover and simmer gently for 20 minutes.

Make 3 slits in the mackerels on either side, to help the flavours to penetrate the flesh. Put in a large baking dish and pour over the hot court bouillon. Cook in a preheated oven at 150°C (300°F) Gas 2 for 30 minutes. Let cool in the liquid, then cover and refrigerate overnight.

The day of serving, remove the mackerel from the dish and lift the fillets, removing as many bones as possible.

Put the fillets, and most of the onion, in a food processor. Add the butter, parsley and tarragon and blend briefly. Transfer to a serving bowl and stir in the lemon juice, Tabasco and a generous grinding of pepper. Taste and adjust the seasoning.

Refrigerate until firm, then serve with toast or sliced baguette.

rustic pâté with green peppercorns

terrine de campagne au poivre vert

250 g boneless pork shoulder, minced

250 g pork belly, minced

500 g veal, minced

200 g calves' liver, finely chopped

1 egg, beaten

2 shallots, finely chopped

2 garlic cloves, crushed

1 tablespoon coarse sea salt

freshly ground black pepper

2 tablespoons green peppercorns in brine, drained, plus extra for decorating

½ teaspoon ground allspice

3 tablespoons Cognac

a handful of fresh bay leaves (see method)

To serve

French cornichons

unsalted butter

sliced baguette

a rectangular terrine mould, 30 x 11 cm

baking parchment

Serves 10–12

If you've never made your own terrine, try this. It is simplicity itself, and you may never use store-bought pâtés again. If you ask your butcher to grind all the meat, except the liver, then it will be even easier. Serve in slices to begin an informal meal, with plenty of fresh baguette, unsalted butter and French cornichons. It also makes a great sandwich filling.

Put the pork shoulder and belly, veal and liver in a large bowl. Add the egg, shallots, garlic, salt, pepper, green peppercorns, allspice and Cognac and mix well, preferably with your hands.

Fill the mould with the meat mixture, patting to spread evenly. Arrange bay leaves on top of the mould and dot with extra green peppercorns. Set it in a roasting tin and add enough boiling water to come half-way up the sides of the mould. Cover the terrine with foil and bake in a preheated oven at 180°C (350°F) Gas 4 until a knife inserted in the middle is hot to the touch after 30 seconds, about 1½ hours.

Remove from the oven and let cool. When the terrine is at room temperature, cover with baking parchment and weight with a few food cans. Refrigerate, with the weights on top. Leave for at least 1 day, but 3 days is best. The pâté will keep, refrigerated, for 1 week. Bring to room temperature before serving.

main courses

I am utterly addicted to this dish with its buttery-lemony sauce. Sole is a well-crafted fish, both meaty and delicate at the same time, and is very easy to eat, bone-wise. Do not make this for a crowd, because you should eat it straight away and two soles are about all that will fit into the average non-stick frying pan. But it is ideal for a tête-à-tête, weekday or otherwise, when you need something elegant and satisfying, in no time at all. Serve with a nice dry French white, a Chablis, for example.

sole meunière

plain flour

2 soles, about 300 g, skinned and cleaned

40 g unsalted butter

2 tablespoons sunflower oil

fine sea salt

freshly squeezed juice of ½ lemon

To serve

a handful of flat leaf parsley, finely chopped

½ lemon, thinly sliced

Serves 2

Put some flour on a large plate, add the fish, cover with flour on both sides and shake off the excess.

Reserve 2 tablespoons of the butter. Heat the oil and remaining butter over medium-high heat in a non-stick frying pan large enough to hold both fish side by side. When it sizzles, add the sole and cook for about 3 minutes. Turn them over and cook on the other side for 3 minutes. Sprinkle the first side with salt while the second side is cooking.

When the fish is cooked through, transfer to warmed dinner plates and season the second side.

Return the frying pan to the heat, add the remaining 2 tablespoons butter and melt over high heat. When it begins to sizzle, lower the heat and add the lemon juice. Cook, scraping the pan for about 10 seconds; do not let the butter burn. Pour this sauce over the fish and sprinkle with parsley. Serve immediately with sliced lemon.

Roughly translated, the English version of this dish means 'roast from the sea'. A gigot is the leg, usually of lamb, but here it refers to the sturdy, meaty nature of monkfish. Most other fish would be overwhelmed by the robust flavours in this Provençal preparation. There is certainly nothing fishy about this, which makes it ideal for those who are less than enthusiastic about eating food from the sea. Good fishmongers will make sure the thin grey membrane that lies under the skin is removed; but if it isn't, insist that it is, all the way down the tail, because it's a difficult job to do at home.

whole roast monkfish
gigot de mer

1 monkfish tail, about 600 g

about 12 thin slices smoked bacon or pancetta – enough to cover the fish

2 tablespoons extra virgin olive oil

200 g mushrooms, sliced

2 large garlic cloves, crushed

250 ml dry white wine

1 kg tomatoes, skinned, deseeded and chopped

2 tablespoons crème fraîche

a handful of basil leaves, chopped

coarse sea salt and freshly ground black pepper

Serves 4

Preheat the oven to 220°C (425°F) Gas 7. Set the bacon on a work surface with the slices slightly overlapping each other. Put the monkfish on top, belly up. Wrap it in the bacon with the ends overlapping across the belly. Turn it over and set aside.

Heat the oil in a large frying pan. Add the mushrooms and a pinch of salt and cook until browned, 3–5 minutes. Stir in the garlic, then add the wine and cook over high heat for 1 minute. Stir in the tomatoes, salt lightly and simmer gently for 5 minutes.

Pour this tomato sauce into a baking dish just large enough to hold the fish. Set the fish on top and roast for 15 minutes. Lower the temperature to 200°C (400°F) Gas 6 and roast for 30 minutes more. Remove from the oven and put the fish on a plate. Stir the crème fraîche and basil into the tomatoes. Set the monkfish back on top and serve.

Sea bass and fennel are virtually inseparable in Provençal cuisine. The market fish stalls of the south always have a plentiful supply of gleaming silvery bass, and fennel grows wild all over the countryside, so it's no wonder. Saffron and harissa, a spicy Tunisian chilli paste, are not traditional, but recipes and ingredients from the former French colonies in North Africa are now found all over France, especially in the south. Serve with a Bandol rosé.

braised sea bass and fennel with saffron and harissa
bar braisé au fenouil epicé

3 tablespoons extra virgin olive oil

1 onion, thinly sliced

3 large fennel bulbs, quartered and thinly sliced

500 ml fresh fish stock

a large pinch of saffron threads

2 small sea bass, cleaned, scaled and heads removed if preferred

250 g red potatoes, peeled and boiled

1–2 teaspoons harissa paste

coarse sea salt

Serves 2

Heat the oil in a large sauté pan with a lid. Add the onion and fennel and cook until lightly golden brown, about 5 minutes. Season lightly with salt.

Add the fish stock and saffron, cover and simmer gently for 15 minutes.

Season the fish inside and out. Put the fish on top of the fennel, cover and simmer gently until the fish is cooked through, 10–15 minutes.

Meanwhile, coarsely crush the potatoes with a fork and set aside.

Remove the fish, set them on large dinner plates and keep them warm in a low oven. Raise the heat and cook the fennel mixture over high heat for 5 minutes. Add the crushed potatoes and harissa and continue cooking, covered, until warmed through, about 5 minutes more. Taste and adjust the seasoning, then spoon onto the plates beside the fish and serve.

Variation Replace the crushed potatoes with couscous, but serve alongside the fish and vegetables instead of mixing it in; stir the harissa into the fennel before serving. For the couscous, follow the packet instructions for the serving size and cooking time.

A traditional dish from the Basque region, where tuna abounds and chillies are appreciated more than in other parts of France. This is quick to prepare and doesn't require long simmering, perfect when you want something hearty and full of flavour in about an hour.

tuna stew with chillies and potatoes
thon marmitako

80 ml extra virgin olive oil

2 onions, sliced

3 green peppers, halved, deseeded and sliced

3 red peppers, halved, deseeded and sliced

750 g red tuna steaks, cut into 5 cm pieces

3 large, hot green chillies, deseeded and sliced

4 ripe tomatoes, skinned, deseeded and chopped

4 garlic cloves, crushed

1 kg medium new potatoes, peeled and sliced into wedges

1 bottle dry white wine

coarse sea salt and freshly ground black pepper

Serves 4

Heat the oil in a large casserole. Add the onions and peppers and cook over high heat until brown, 3–5 minutes. Remove from the pan to a bowl, season with salt and pepper. Add the tuna and chillies to the pan, cooking to sear, 3–5 minutes. Add the tomatoes, garlic and potatoes, then add salt to taste and stir carefully.

Return the onion mixture to the pan and pour in the wine. Add 250 ml water. Bring to the boil and boil for 1 minute, then reduce the heat, cover and simmer gently until the potatoes are cooked through, 30–35 minutes. Serve immediately.

Salt cod and snails are traditional ingredients in this Provençal dish, but salmon and prawns are easier to come by for most people. Be sure to use very good oil; despite great quantities of garlic, the flavour base of the aïöli comes from the oil, so it is worth investing in something special. Serve for a crowd, with everything freshly cooked and warmish, or at room temperature. Wash it all down with a chilled white or rosé from Provence.

le grand aïöli

4 tablespoons extra virgin olive oil

4 salmon steaks

200 g unpeeled prawn tails

300 g small new potatoes

100 g asparagus tips

1 fresh bay leaf

6 baby carrots, sliced lengthways

1 cauliflower, broken into florets

1 broccoli, broken into florets

200 g baby courgettes, halved lengthwise

6 eggs

200 g small green beans

150 g cherry tomatoes

4 cooked beetroot

coarse sea salt

Aïöli

2 egg yolks

about 400 ml best-quality extra virgin olive oil

6 large garlic cloves

fine sea salt

Serves 6

Heat 1 tablespoon of the oil in a large non-stick frying pan, add the salmon and cook for about 3 minutes on each side, or until just cooked through. Season with salt and set aside. Add another 1 tablespoon of the oil to the pan. When hot, add the prawns and cook until pink and firm, 3–5 minutes. Do not overcook or they will be tough. Season and set aside.

Put the potatoes in a saucepan with cold water to cover and bring to the boil. When the water boils, add salt and cook until tender, 15–20 minutes. Drain and set aside. Meanwhile, cook the asparagus tips and beans in boiling salted water until just tender, about 3 minutes.

Bring a saucepan of water to the boil with the bay leaf. When it boils, add the carrots and cook until *al dente*, 3–4 minutes. Remove with a slotted spoon and set aside. Return the water to the boil, add the cauliflower florets and cook until just tender, about 5 minutes. Remove with a slotted spoon. Return the water to the boil, add the broccoli and cook until just tender, 3–4 minutes.

Rub the courgettes all over with the remaining oil. Heat a ridged stove-top grill pan. When hot, add the courgette pieces and cook, about 4 minutes per side. Alternatively, cook the same way in a non-stick pan. Remove and season.

Put the eggs in a saucepan with cold water to cover. Bring to the boil and cook for 6 minutes from boiling point. Drain, cool under running water, then peel and slice.

To make the aïöli, put the egg yolks in a small, deep bowl. Whisk well, then gradually whisk in the oil, adding it bit by bit and whisking vigorously, until the mixture is as thick as mayonnaise. Stir in the garlic and season to taste.

Arrange all the vegetables and fish on a single platter, or on several platters. Serve, passing the aïöli separately.

Large bowls of steaming hot mussels are served in bistros all over France. The classic recipe is *à la marinière*, with shallots and white wine. My combination of ingredients evolved because I could eat mussels every day, just steamed plain, but my husband does not share this enthusiasm. If, however, they come in a garlicky, saffron-scented sauce, reminiscent of summer holidays, then everyone is happy.

mussels with fennel, tomatoes, garlic and saffron
moules à la bouillabaisse

2 tablespoons extra virgin olive oil

1 small onion, chopped

½ fennel bulb, chopped

4 garlic cloves, crushed

250 ml dry white wine

400 g canned chopped tomatoes

a pinch of saffron threads

1 kg fresh mussels

coarse sea salt and freshly ground black pepper

a handful of flat leaf parsley, chopped, to serve

Serves 4

Heat the oil in a large sauté pan. Add the onion and fennel and cook until soft, 3–5 minutes. Add the garlic, wine and tomatoes. Boil for 1 minute, then lower the heat, add the saffron and a pinch of salt. Simmer gently for 15 minutes.

Just before serving, clean and debeard the mussels, discarding any that do not close. (To prepare mussels, see note on page 21.)

Raise the heat under the sauce and, when boiling, add the prepared mussels. Cover and cook until the mussels open, 2–3 minutes. Discard any that do not open. Serve immediately, sprinkled with parsley.

Variation Frites are the classic accompaniments for mussels when served as a main course. See the recipe on page 79.

On a recent visit to France, we went to the elegant seaside town of Hossegor. We window-shopped around the centre, then strolled through the back streets, trying to choose which villa we would buy when we won the lottery. By the time we got to the seafront, we were famished. The first restaurant we saw had *chipirons à l'ail* written on the blackboard so we sat down, ordered some, and had a most memorable meal. *Chipirons* are tiny squid, very sweet and delicate, and unavailable where I live, but prawns are a good substitute. Serve with lots of bread to mop up the garlicky sauce.

garlic prawns
crevettes à l'ail

125 ml olive oil

1 kg prawn tails, with shells

8–10 garlic cloves, chopped

a large handful of flat leaf parsley, chopped

coarse sea salt and freshly ground black pepper

1 lemon, cut into wedges, to serve

Serves 4

Heat the oil in a large sauté pan. When hot but not smoking, add the prawns and garlic and cook until the prawns turn pink, 3–5 minutes. Be careful not to let the garlic burn. Remove from the heat, sprinkle with salt, freshly ground black pepper and parsley and mix well. Serve immediately, with lemon wedges.

This poor man's version of a dish in which truffle slices are stuffed under the chicken skin makes a nice change from ordinary roast chicken. The perfume of bay leaves and thyme delicately flavours the chicken flesh, while the tartness of the lemon keeps it lively.

roast chicken with bay leaves, thyme and lemon
poulet rôti aux herbes et citron

1 free-range chicken, preferably organic, about 1.5 kg

2 unwaxed lemons, preferably organic, 1 quartered, 1 sliced

6 large fresh bay leaves

2 sprigs of thyme

1–2 tablespoons extra virgin olive oil or 30 g butter

1 teaspoon dried thyme

1 onion, sliced in rounds

250 ml dry white wine (optional)

1 tablespoon unsalted butter

coarse sea salt

a roasting tin with a rack

Serves 4

Season the inside of the chicken generously and stuff with the lemon quarters, 2 of the bay leaves and the thyme.

Using your fingers, separate the skin from the breast meat to create a little pocket and put 1 bay leaf on each side of the breast, underneath the skin. Put the remaining 2 bay leaves under the skin of the thighs. Rub the outside of the chicken all over with oil or butter, season generously and sprinkle all over with the dried thyme.

Put the chicken on its side on a rack set over a roasting tin. Add water to fill the bottom of the tin by about 1 cm and add the sliced lemon and onion. Cook in a preheated oven at 220°C (425°F) Gas 7 for 40 minutes, then turn the chicken on its other side. Continue roasting the chicken until cooked through and the juices run clear when a thigh is pierced with a skewer, about 40 minutes more. Add extra water to the tin if necessary during cooking.

Remove from the oven, remove the chicken from the rack to a plate and let stand, covered, for 10 minutes. Add 250 ml water, or the wine if using, to the pan juices and cook over high heat, scraping the bottom of the tin, 3–5 minutes. Stir in the butter. Carve the chicken and serve with the pan juices.

Like all traditional dishes, there are many versions of this recipe; some call only for green peppers, some use only onions and chillies. I think chillies are imperative, and if you want to be completely authentic, use *piment d'Espelette*, which is a most delicious little chilli grown in the Basque region of France, but very difficult to find outside this area. They are pleasantly spicy without being overpowering, so whatever chilli you use, resist the temptation to overdo it. Serve with rice.

chicken with peppers, onions, ham and tomatoes
poulet basquaise

2 tablespoons extra virgin olive oil

1 free-range chicken, about 2 kg, cut into 8 pieces

2 onions, sliced

2 red peppers, halved, deseeded and sliced

2 yellow peppers, halved, deseeded and sliced

2–4 large garlic cloves, crushed

2 small hot green chillies, deseeded and thinly sliced (or ½ teaspoon crushed dried chillies)

1 thick slice jambon de Bayonne or other unsmoked ham, about 2 cm thick and 160 g, cut into strips

1 kg ripe tomatoes, skinned, deseeded and chopped

coarse sea salt and freshly ground black pepper

Serves 4

Heat the oil in a large sauté pan with a lid, add the chicken pieces skin side down and cook until brown, 5–10 minutes. Don't crowd the pan; if you can't fit all the pieces at once, brown in batches. Transfer the chicken to a plate, season well with salt and set aside.

Add the onions and peppers to the pan, season with salt and black pepper, then cook over medium heat until soft, 15–20 minutes. Stir in the garlic, chillies and ham and cook for 1 minute. Add the tomatoes, mix well, then add all the chicken pieces and bury them under the sauce. Cover and cook over low heat until the chicken is tender, 30–40 minutes. Taste for seasoning after 20 minutes. This dish can be made in advance and even improves after a night in the refrigerator.

Poulet sauté is at home all over France, but I especially like this south-eastern version with its assertive flavours. It goes well with rice or fresh pasta such as the saffron tagliatelle used here, and a sturdy red wine, such as a Collioure or Minervois.

chicken with tomato, garlic and olives
poulet sauté niçoise

2 tablespoons extra virgin olive oil

1 free-range chicken, about 2 kg, cut into 6–8 pieces

8 garlic cloves, finely chopped

400 g canned chopped tomatoes

a pinch of sugar

50 g black olives, preferably niçoise, pitted and coarsely chopped

coarse sea salt and freshly ground black pepper

a bunch of fresh basil, torn

Serves 4–6

Heat 1 tablespoon of the oil in a large sauté pan. Add the chicken pieces and brown on all sides. Transfer the chicken to a plate, salt generously and set aside. Add the remaining oil and garlic and cook for 1 minute; do not let it burn. Add the tomatoes and sugar. Stir well and return the chicken pieces to the pan. Cover and simmer gently until the chicken is cooked, 25–30 minutes.

Transfer the chicken pieces to a serving dish, then raise the heat and cook the sauce to thicken slightly, about 10 minutes. Add salt and pepper to taste, then stir in the olives. Pour the sauce over the chicken pieces, sprinkle with the basil and serve immediately.

A dish without a region, this is served pretty much all over France, in homes as well as restaurants. It's quick to make, if you get your butcher to cut up the chicken, and the flavour of tarragon lifts this out of the ordinary. Make this dish midweek and you'll have a lovely supper on the table in under an hour, or serve it for your next dinner party and it will seem like you slaved away all day. A red St-Estèphe or Ladoix would be the ideal wine.

chicken with tarragon
poulet sauté à l'estragon

I tablespoon unsalted butter

I tablespoon sunflower oil

I free-range corn-fed chicken, about 2 kg, cut into 6–8 pieces

2 carrots, chopped

I shallot or ½ small onion, chopped

a sprig of thyme

2–3 sprigs of flat leaf parsley

a bunch of tarragon

3 tablespoons crème fraîche

coarse sea salt and freshly ground black pepper

Serves 4

Melt the butter and oil in a large sauté pan with a lid. Add the chicken pieces and cook until brown, about 5 minutes. Work in batches if your pan is not big enough. Put the browned chicken pieces on a plate and season well with salt and pepper.

Add the carrots and shallot and cook, stirring for a minute or so. Return the chicken to the pan and add water to cover half-way. Add the thyme, parsley and a few sprigs of tarragon. Cover and simmer gently for 30 minutes.

Meanwhile, strip the leaves from the remaining tarragon, chop them finely and set aside. Add the stems to the cooking chicken.

Remove the chicken from the pan and put in a serving dish. Remove and discard the tarragon stems. (The recipe can be prepared a few hours in advance up to this point, then completed just before serving.)

Raise the heat and cook the sauce until reduced by half. Strain and return the sauce to the pan. Stir in the crème fraîche and the chopped tarragon. Heat briefly (do not boil) and pour over the chicken. Serve immediately.

If you can find a true guinea fowl, from a butcher or specialist supplier, then this will taste as it should (see Mail Order and Websites, page 142). It is worth the effort to search out the real thing because supermarket guinea fowl is disappointing, to say the least. The flavour bears no resemblance to anything worth paying money for; you are better off buying an organic or free-range chicken, since the preparation is the same and the result will be superior. Fortunately, the lentils will never disappoint.

guinea fowl with lentils
pintade aux lentilles

1 guinea fowl, about 1.5 kg

3 tablespoons extra virgin olive oil

225 g dried green lentils, preferably French

a sprig of thyme

1 fresh bay leaf

4 large shallots, chopped

2 carrots, chopped

150 g bacon lardons

250 ml dry white wine

coarse sea salt and freshly ground black pepper

a roasting tin fitted with a rack

Serves 4

Rub the guinea fowl all over with 1 tablespoon of the olive oil and season well, inside and out. Put on a rack set in a roasting tin and cook in a preheated oven at 220°C (425°F) Gas 7 until browned and the juices run clear when the thigh is pierced with a skewer, about 1 hour.

Meanwhile, put the lentils, thyme and bay leaf into a saucepan and just cover with water. Bring to the boil, reduce the heat, cover with a lid and simmer gently until tender, about 25 minutes. Drain and season with ½ teaspoon salt.

Heat the remaining 2 tablespoons oil in a frying pan. Add the shallots and carrots and cook until just tender, 3–5 minutes. Stir in the bacon lardons and cook, stirring, until well browned. Add the wine and cook over high heat until reduced by half. Add the lentils, discard the herbs and set aside.

Remove the guinea fowl from the oven and let stand for 10 minutes. Carve into serving pieces and serve immediately, with the lentils.

If you can find imported French duck magrets, they are worth getting, both for the flavour and for the size. If you use domestic duck breasts, cooking time will be less and you will probably need 2 per person. Serve with sautéed or roasted potatoes and a red wine such as Madiran.

duck breasts
with peppercorns
magret de canard aux deux poivres

2 French duck magrets or 4 duck breasts, about 650 g

3 tablespoons Cognac

200 ml crème fraîche

1 tablespoon coarsely ground black pepper

1 tablespoon green peppercorns in brine, drained

coarse sea salt

Serves 2

Trim the excess fat from around the duck breasts, then score the skin in a diamond pattern.

Heat a heavy frying pan. When hot, add the duck skin side first and cook 7–8 minutes. Turn and cook the other side 4–5 minutes, depending on thickness. Remove from the pan, season with salt and keep them warm.

Drain almost all the fat from the pan. Return to the heat and add the Cognac, scraping the bottom of the pan. Stir in the cream, black pepper and green peppercorns. Cook for 1 minute.

Slice the duck diagonally lengthways and put on plates. Pour the sauce over the top and serve immediately.

Rabbit and prunes don't really have a season, but this somehow seems autumnal, just the thing when the days are getting shorter and cooler, and it's nice to fill the house with appetizing aromas. A more apt name would be Drunken Rabbit, because there is so much wine, Cognac and port. But prunes it is, and they do play a vital part, adding a pleasant sweetness to the rich, velvety sauce and salty bacon lardons. Serve it with fresh pasta tossed in butter – tagliatelle is ideal. Chicken can be substituted for the rabbit, but don't cook it as long.

rabbit with prunes
lapin aux pruneaux

1 rabbit, cut into 7–8 pieces

2 tablespoons sunflower oil

30 g unsalted butter

2 onions, halved and sliced

200 g bacon lardons

about 100 g plain flour

125 ml port

400 g plump prunes, preferably French

1 tablespoon crème fraîche

coarse sea salt and freshly ground black pepper

Marinade

1 onion, chopped

1 carrot, chopped

2 garlic cloves, crushed

2 sprigs of thyme

1 fresh bay leaf

1 bottle red wine, 750 ml

250 ml Cognac

a few peppercorns

Serves 4

One day before serving, mix all the marinade ingredients in a ceramic or glass bowl. Add the rabbit pieces, cover and refrigerate overnight.

When ready to cook, remove the rabbit from the marinade, strain the liquid and reserve. Discard all the vegetables but keep the thyme and bay leaf. Pat the rabbit pieces dry with kitchen paper.

Heat 1 tablespoon of the oil and half the butter in a casserole. Add the onions and bacon lardons and cook over high heat until brown, 5 minutes. Remove and set aside.

Put the flour on a plate and add the rabbit pieces, turning to coat lightly. Add the remaining oil and butter to the casserole and heat. When sizzling, put the rabbit pieces in the casserole and brown all over. Pour in the strained marinade liquid, bacon and onion mixture and port. Add the reserved thyme and bay leaf and season with salt and pepper. Bring to the boil, skim off the foam, then lower the heat, cover and simmer for 45 minutes. Taste for seasoning.

Remove the rabbit pieces to a plate, add the prunes, raise the heat and cook until thickened, 10–15 minutes more. Stir in the crème fraîche, return the rabbit to the casserole and cook just to warm through; do not boil. Serve immediately.

marinated pork roast
rôti de porc mariné

1 bottle dry white wine, 750 ml

50 ml white wine vinegar

1 large onion, sliced

2 carrots, sliced

1 fresh bay leaf

a sprig of thyme

1 celery stalk, with leaves

2 garlic cloves, sliced

1 teaspoon peppercorns

2 tablespoons coarse sea salt

2–3 fresh sage leaves

1 boneless pork loin roast, about 1.5 kg

Serves 4–6

If you thought pork was bland, think again. It is actually a spectacular vehicle for all sorts of flavours, and responds remarkably well to marinating. The French have known this for years, because the idea for this recipe came from one of my favourite cookbooks, *La Cuisine de Mme Saint-Ange*, first published in 1927. Any cut of pork can be marinated, from a few hours to overnight, and the leftovers are as good, if not better, than the original. Serve with something creamy, like Cauliflower Gratin (page 109), or roasted vegetables.

Two days before serving, mix all the ingredients in a large ceramic or glass bowl. Cover and refrigerate for 2 days, turning the pork regularly.

When ready to cook, remove the pork from the marinade and put it in a roasting tin. Add the vegetables and flavourings from the marinade. Cook in a preheated oven at 200°C (400°F) Gas 6, basting occasionally with the marinade liquid, for 1½ hours. Serve immediately.

If it has apples and cream, then it must be from Normandy. The cider is a good clue as well, and it provides a luxuriously rich sauce for the long-simmered pork. Unlike recipes from more southerly realms, this is subtle and delicate, but no less powerful for its discretion. A good dish for all the family, as children (and adults) enjoy sweet things to accompany their meat. Serve with the cider used in cooking, or a red wine from the Loire.

pork in cider with potatoes and apples
porc au cidre aux deux pommes

30 g unsalted butter

2 onions, sliced

1 tablespoon sunflower oil

1 pork middle leg roast, about 1.75 kg

1.5 litres dry cider

2 sprigs of thyme

800 g medium new potatoes, peeled and halved lengthways

125 ml double cream

coarse sea salt and freshly ground black pepper

Apples

60 g unsalted butter

5 tart apples, such as Braeburn or Cox's, peeled, cored and sliced

Serves 4

Melt the butter in a large casserole. Add the onions and cook gently until softened but not browned, about 5 minutes. Remove the onions. Add the oil, raise the heat, add the pork and cook until browned all over. Remove and season well.

Add some of the cider, heat and scrape the bottom of the pan. Return the meat, onions, remaining cider and thyme. Season lightly with salt and pepper and bring to the boil. Boil for 1 minute, skim off any foam that rises to the surface, then lower the heat, cover and cook in a preheated oven at 150°C (300°F) Gas 2 for 4 hours. Turn the pork regularly, and taste and adjust the seasoning half-way through cooking.

One hour before the end of the cooking time, add the potatoes and continue cooking.

Remove from the oven, transfer the pork and potatoes to a plate and cover with foil to keep it warm. Cook the sauce over high heat to reduce slightly, 10–15 minutes. Taste.

Meanwhile, to cook the apples, melt the butter in a large frying pan, add the apples and cook over high heat until browned and tender, 5–10 minutes. Do not crowd the pan; use 2 pans if necessary.

To serve, slice the pork and arrange on plates with the potatoes and apples. Stir the cream into the sauce and serve immediately.

This is the sort of basic fare you'll find in cafés and bistros all over France. The mustardy-vinegary sauce is ideal with pork. Cornichons are the best part so be sure to use the real thing. They must be small and, ideally, bottled in France. I've seen other tiny gherkins labelled as cornichons but, unless they come from France, they never taste as I expect. Serve with mashed potatoes.

pork chops with piquant sauce
côtes de porc charcutière

4 thick-cut pork chops, rind removed

extra virgin olive oil

coarse sea salt and freshly ground black pepper

Mustard and vinegar sauce

60 ml wine, dry white or red

250 ml fresh chicken stock

60 ml tarragon or sherry vinegar

40 g unsalted butter

3 shallots, finely chopped

1 tablespoon plain flour

2 teaspoons tomato purée

1 teaspoon coarse Dijon mustard

8 French cornichons, sliced into rounds

a sprig of tarragon, leaves stripped and chopped

a small handful of flat leaf parsley, chopped

Serves 2–4

To make the sauce, put the wine and stock in a small saucepan. Bring to the boil for 1 minute, then stir in the vinegar. Set aside.

Melt the butter in another saucepan. Add the shallots and cook until soft, 3–5 minutes. Add the flour and cook, stirring for 1 minute. Add the warm stock mixture, tomato purée and mix well. Simmer gently for 15 minutes.

Meanwhile, to cook the pork chops, rub a ridged stove-top grill pan with the oil and heat on high. When hot, add the pork chops and cook for 4–5 minutes. Turn and cook the other side for 3–4 minutes. Remove from the heat and season on both sides with salt and pepper.

Stir the mustard, cornichons, tarragon and parsley into the sauce and serve immediately, with the pork chops.

cassoulet

A classic from the south-west, adapted for those of us outside France. Do not let the long list put you off. This is actually quite easy: cook the beans, cook the meat stew, brown the duck and sausages, then put it all together. That's it. You do need good sausages, with as high a pork content as possible. Duck confit is sold canned in large supermarkets, or in good delicatessens. You will also need several large pots, a large dish to cook it in and very hungry friends.

Beans

850 g dried haricot beans

300 g thick sliced unsmoked middle bacon

rind from 4 thick pork chops

1 carrot, chopped

1 fresh bay leaf

1 onion, studded with 2 cloves

4 whole garlic cloves

1 teaspoon salt

Meat

1 tablespoon extra virgin olive oil

750 g pork spare ribs

750 g boneless lamb shoulder, cubed

1 onion, chopped

3 garlic cloves, crushed

400 g canned chopped tomatoes

1 fresh bay leaf

2 litres fresh chicken stock

6 canned duck confit thigh pieces

10 Toulouse sausages or other pure pork sausages

breadcrumbs

coarse sea salt and freshly ground black pepper

Serves 8

In the morning, one day before serving, put the beans in a bowl with plenty of cold water and let soak (soak for at least 6 hours, or start 2 days early and soak overnight).

Drain the beans. Put in a large saucepan with cold water to cover, bring to the boil and simmer for 10 minutes. Drain. Return the beans to the pan and add the bacon, pork rind, carrot, bay leaf, onion and garlic. Cover with water by about 5 cm and bring to the boil. Lower the heat and simmer gently for 1 hour. Add the 1 teaspoon salt and continue cooking for 30 minutes more. Let cool, then refrigerate overnight; do not drain.

Meanwhile, to prepare the meat stew, heat the oil in a large frying pan. Add the pork and lamb and fry until brown. Add the onion and garlic and cook until just soft, about 3 minutes. Add the tomatoes, bay leaf and stock. Season. Bring to the boil, skim off the foam, then lower the heat, cover and simmer gently for 1½ hours. Add salt and pepper to taste. Let cool and refrigerate overnight.

The next day, about 3 hours before serving, discard the fat from the top of the stew. Remove the meat from the spare ribs, return to the stew and discard the bones. Bring the beans to room temperature (or warm slightly), drain and reserve the liquid. Season to taste.

Heat a large frying pan, add the duck confit pieces and fry until browned. Remove, cut the thighs into pieces and set aside. In the same pan, brown the sausages. Do not discard the cooking fat.

Now you are ready to assemble. Remove the pork rind and bacon from the beans and put in a large casserole dish. Top with one-third of the beans. Arrange the duck confit in the middle (so that you know where to find it when serving), and the sausages all around the edge. Spread the meat stew on top. Cover with the remaining beans. Spoon in some of the reserved bean liquid (you should just be able to see it), then sprinkle with a thin layer of breadcrumbs. Pour in the duck and sausage fat. Cook in a preheated oven at 220°C (425°F) Gas 7 for 30 minutes.

Reduce the heat to 190°C (375°F) Gas 5. Gently break up the crust on top, then spoon over some more bean liquid and sprinkle with more breadcrumbs. Continue checking, about every 30 minutes or so, adding more liquid as necessary; be sure not to let the cassoulet dry out. When the crust is well browned and the cassoulet has cooked for 2 hours, remove from the oven.

Serve hot, with a portion of confit, the sausages and plenty of beans for each guest.

Nothing says 'bistro' better than this. The shallot butter is a fancy flourish; it is just as authentic to serve as is, with nothing more than Dijon mustard, for both the steak and the frites (but no ketchup, please!) The secret of cooking great frites is to use a good floury variety of potato and to cook them twice. They should be dry, rustling, crisp and well seasoned.

steak and frites
steak frites

4 sirloin or rib eye steaks, about 300 g each, 3 cm thick

1 tablespoon sunflower oil

coarse sea salt and freshly ground black pepper

Shallot butter

100 g unsalted butter, softened

2 shallots, finely chopped

150 ml red wine

a large sprig of tarragon

several sprigs of flat leaf parsley

1 teaspoon coarse sea salt

½ teaspoon coarsely ground black pepper

Frites

500 g floury potatoes (for baking and frying)

sunflower oil, for frying

sea salt, to serve

a large saucepan with frying basket, or electric deep-fryer

Serves 4

To make the shallot butter, put about 25 g of the butter in a saucepan and melt over low heat. Add the shallots and cook until softened. Add the wine, bring to the boil and cook until syrupy and the wine has almost completely evaporated. Set aside to cool.

Put the cooled shallots, remaining butter, tarragon, parsley, salt and pepper in a small food processor and blend briefly. Transfer the mixture to a piece of baking parchment and shape into a log. Roll up and chill until firm.

To prepare the frites, peel the potatoes and cut into 5 mm slices. Cut the slices into 5 mm strips. Put into a bowl of iced water for at least 5 minutes. When ready to cook, drain and pat dry with kitchen paper.

Fill a large saucepan one-third full with the oil, or if using a deep-fryer to the manufacturer's recommended level. Heat the oil to 190°C (375°F) or until a cube of bread will brown in 30 seconds. Working in batches, put 2 large handfuls of potato strips into the frying basket, lower carefully into the oil and fry for about 4 minutes. Remove and drain on kitchen paper. Repeat until all the strips have been cooked. Skim any debris off the top of the oil, reheat to the same temperature, then fry the strips for a second time until crisp and golden, about 2 minutes. Remove and drain on kitchen paper, then sprinkle with salt. Keep hot in the oven until ready to serve

To prepare the steaks, rub them on both sides with the oil. Heat a ridged stove-top grill pan. When hot, add the steaks and cook for 1½–2 minutes. Turn and cook the other side for 1–2 minutes. This will produce a rare steak. To produce a medium-rare steak, turn and cook again on both sides for 2–3 minutes more.

Remove from the pan and season both sides. Let stand for a few minutes. Serve with rounds of the butter and the frites.

The sailors who used to guide barges up and down the Rhône, from Arles to Lyon, were lucky men indeed. They invented this dish and, I assume, ate it often. If I were having my last supper, this would be it, with mashed potatoes, a green salad and a good red Rhône wine.

braised steak with anchovies and capers
brouffade

150 ml extra virgin olive oil

8 garlic cloves, crushed

a small handful of flat leaf parsley, chopped

1 teaspoon coarsely ground black pepper

1 fresh bay leaf

a sprig of thyme

1 inner stalk of celery, with leaves

4 thick rump steaks, about 300 g each

4 onions, halved and sliced

3 tablespoons capers, drained

12 cornichons, chopped

10 anchovy fillets packed in oil, finely chopped

1 tablespoon plain flour

3 tablespoons red wine vinegar

Serves 4–6

One day before serving, mix the oil, garlic, parsley, pepper, bay leaf, thyme and celery in a shallow dish. Add the steaks and turn to coat well with the mixture. Cover with plastic wrap and refrigerate overnight, turning at least twice.

Put the onions, capers and cornichons in a bowl and toss well.

Put the anchovies and flour in a small bowl and blend well. Remove the meat from the marinade and stir in the anchovy mixture and vinegar.

Choose a lidded ovenproof casserole, deep and just wide enough to hold 2 steaks side-by-side. Put one-third of the onion mixture in the casserole and put 2 steaks on top. Spoon in half of the marinade, spreading it over the meat. Top with half the remaining onions, then the remaining steaks. Spoon over the rest of the marinade and top with the rest of the onions.

Pour in about 250 ml water. Cut a piece of baking parchment to about the diameter of the casserole and put this on top of the onions to help seal in all the juices. Cover with the lid and cook in a preheated oven at 150°C (300°F) Gas 2 for 3 hours. Serve immediately.

This humble French culinary masterpiece rates high on the scale of life's little pleasures. It has no precise geographical origin – everyone makes it, and rightly so. The beef practically melts in your mouth and the broth is rich, sweet and buttery from all the carrots. A prime candidate for potatoes, tagliatelle or, even better, the Macaroni Gratin (page 118). French Beans with Garlic (page 106) would also be delicious. Experiment with different cuts of beef – anything that will stand up to long, slow simmering.

braised beef brisket with carrots
boeuf aux carottes

2 tablespoons extra virgin olive oil
1.5 kg rolled brisket
1.5 kg carrots
150 g bacon lardons
1 onion, halved and sliced
2 garlic cloves, crushed
1 fresh bay leaf
a sprig of thyme
1 small leafy celery stalk
500 ml dry white wine
coarse sea salt and freshly ground black pepper

Serves 4–6

Heat 1 tablespoon of the oil in a large casserole. Add the meat and cook until browned on all sides. Transfer to a plate and sprinkle generously with salt.

Heat the remaining oil in the casserole, add the carrots and 1 teaspoon salt and cook, stirring occasionally until brown, 3–5 minutes. Remove and set aside.

Put the lardons and onion in the casserole and cook over high heat until browned, 3–5 minutes.

Add the garlic, bay leaf, thyme, celery, beef and carrots. Pour in the wine and add water almost to cover. Bring to the boil, skim, then cover with a lid and cook in a preheated oven at 150°C (300°F) Gas 2 for 3 hours. Turn the meat over at least once during cooking.

Sprinkle with pepper and serve with your choice of accompaniments.

This classic dish is a reminder that true bistro food is not about expensive cuts, or elaborate sauces. In fact, the real recipe calls for leftover beef from a stew – home economy at its best. If you have any leftovers from the Braised Beef (page 83), then use them. It's also nice if you mix leftovers, like lamb and pork, with the beef. This summery dish is ideal for lunch or a light supper, served with a green salad and a light-medium red wine.

stuffed tomatoes
tomates farcies

2 tablespoons extra virgin olive oil

4 shallots, finely chopped

3 large gàrlic cloves, crushed

100 g bacon, finely chopped

3 tablespoons dry white wine

12 large tomatoes (not beefsteak)

375 g beef mince

1 egg

4 tablespoons breadcrumbs

½ teaspoon herbes de provence

a handful of flat leaf parsley, finely chopped

coarse sea salt and freshly ground black pepper

a baking dish, greased with 2 tablespoons olive oil

Serves 4–6

Heat the oil in a frying pan. Add the shallots and garlic and cook until softened but not browned, 3–5 minutes. Add the bacon lardons and fry until just beginning to brown, 3–5 minutes. Stir in the wine and cook until evaporated. Transfer to a bowl and let cool.

Slice off the tops of the tomatoes and set the tops aside. Carefully deseed with a spoon. Pat the insides dry with kitchen paper and season with salt and pepper. Set aside.

Add the beef to the shallot mixture, then stir in the egg, breadcrumbs, herbs, parsley and 1 teaspoon salt. Cook a small piece of the stuffing mixture in a frying pan, taste for seasoning, adding more salt if needed.

Fill the tomato shells with the beef mixture, mounding it at the top. Replace the tomato tops and arrange apart in the prepared baking dish. Cook in a preheated oven at 200°C (400°F) Gas 6 until cooked through and browned, about 30 minutes.

Variation Another speciality from Provence, *les petits farcis* (little stuffed vegetables), can be made using the same stuffing to fill a variety of vegetables: courgettes, aubergines and peppers are ideal, but you can also use artichokes and mushrooms. Provençal dishes often have a breadcrumb topping, so add a handful of chopped fresh parsley, crushed garlic and some grated Parmesan to fresh breadcrumbs and sprinkle over the tops before baking.

30 g unsalted butter
or 2 tablespoons sunflower oil

2 onions, chopped

2 garlic cloves

750 g beef mince

70 g bacon, finely chopped

125 ml dry white wine

a handful of flat leaf parsley, chopped

a sprig of thyme, leaves stripped

2 tablespoons tomato purée

50 g freshly grated Gruyère cheese

coarse sea salt and freshly
ground black pepper

Potato purée

2 kg potatoes

1 fresh bay leaf

250 ml hot milk

100 g unsalted butter, cut into pieces

sea salt

a baking dish, about 30 cm long,
greased with butter

Serves 4–6

Antoine-Augustin Parmentier introduced potatoes to the French public in the late 18th century, and this dish of minced beef nestled between two layers of creamy mashed potatoes is a tribute to him. Not as glamorous as a bridge over the Seine perhaps, but delicious nonetheless. The traditional recipe calls for leftover cooked beef, specifically stewed or boiled beef, so use that if you have some. The taste benefits from flavourful leftovers, but mince that has been well seasoned and cooked in a bit of wine comes a close second. Serve with a fruity red wine.

beef and potato gratin
hachis parmentier

To prepare the purée, put the potatoes and bay leaf in a saucepan of cold water. Bring to the boil, add salt and cook until tender. Drain.

Put the potatoes in a large bowl and mash coarsely with a wooden spoon. Using an electric mixer, gradually add the milk and butter, beating until the mixture is smooth. Add salt and whisk well. If the potatoes are very dry, add more milk. Taste, then add more butter and/or salt as necessary and set aside.

Heat the butter in a frying pan, add the onions and cook over high heat until just brown, 3–5 minutes. Add the garlic, beef and chopped bacon and cook until almost completely browned. Add the wine and cook until almost evaporated. Stir in the parsley, thyme leaves and tomato purée. Taste and adjust the seasoning with salt and pepper.

Spread half the potatoes in the prepared baking dish. Add the beef mixture and level with a spoon. Spread with the remaining potatoes. Sprinkle with the cheese and bake in a preheated oven at 200°C (400°F) Gas 6 until golden, about 25–30 minutes.

Gasconnade refers to the anchovies and it is a traditional way of flavouring lamb in the south-west of France. The long, slow cooking in wine mellows the anchovies, making for an intensely rich sauce and very tender meat. Serve with fresh tagliatelle, potatoes or flageolet beans.

leg of lamb
with anchovies
agneau à la gasconnade

I leg of lamb, about 1.5 kg, trimmed

14 anchovy fillets

2 tablespoons extra virgin olive oil

2 onions, chopped

2 carrots, chopped

3 garlic cloves, crushed

2 tomatoes, skinned, deseeded and chopped

I bottle red wine, 750 ml

2 sprigs of thyme

I fresh bay leaf

I tablespoon tomato purée

coarse sea salt

Serves 4–6

Make slits all over the lamb and insert the anchovy fillets, as you do when studding with garlic.

Heat the oil in a lidded casserole just large enough to hold the lamb comfortably. Add the lamb and brown on all sides. Remove, season lightly and set aside.

Put the onions and carrots in the casserole and cook over high heat until lightly browned, about 3–5 minutes. Add the crushed garlic and chopped tomatoes and cook for 1 minute. Add the wine, sprigs of thyme, bay leaf and tomato purée and bring to the boil. Boil for 1 minute, then add the lamb. Cover with the lid, transfer to a preheated oven at 180°C (350°F) Gas 4 and cook for 1½ hours, turning every 20 minutes or so. Remove the thyme and bay leaf and serve.

This reminds me of long Sunday family lunches, the ones that go on almost until dinner, the likes of which I'd never known before living in France. To re-create something similar, start with apéritifs and nibbles at midday, then serve this with boiled baby new potatoes and a bottle of St-Emilion. Follow with a green salad and a generous cheese platter. An apple tart (page 132) before coffee makes the perfect ending. A lovely way to herald in the spring.

spring lamb stew with vegetables
navarin d'agneau

1 tablespoon sunflower oil

700 g lamb neck fillet, cubed

500 g lamb chump chops, each one cut into several pieces

1 tablespoon plain flour

2 ripe tomatoes, skinned, deseeded and chopped

2 garlic cloves, crushed

600 ml fresh lamb or chicken stock

1 fresh bay leaf

a sprig of thyme

4 baby carrots, cut into 3 cm pieces

200 g baby leeks, cut into 5 cm lengths

200 g baby turnips

200 g sugar snap peas

a handful of flat leaf parsley, chopped

coarse sea salt and freshly ground black pepper

Serves 4

Heat the oil in a large casserole, add the lamb and brown the pieces on all sides, in batches if necessary. When all the lamb has been browned, return it all to the pan, lower the heat slightly and stir in a pinch of salt and the flour. Cook, stirring to coat evenly, for 1 minute.

Add the tomatoes and garlic. Stir in the stock, bay leaf and thyme. Bring to the boil and skim off any foam that rises to the surface. Reduce the heat, then cover and simmer gently for 40 minutes.

Add the carrots, leeks and turnips and cook for 25 minutes more. Taste and adjust the seasoning with salt and pepper.

Add the peas and cook for 7 minutes. Sprinkle with the parsley and serve immediately.

vegetables

Poor old celery; it is more often an ingredient than the star of a dish. However, in this traditional Provençal recipe, it takes centre stage. Beef is the ideal complement to the trinity of celery, tomatoes and anchovies, so serve this with roast beef or grilled steaks.

braised celery
céleri braisé

2 whole bunches of celery

2 tablespoons extra virgin olive oil

75 g bacon lardons

1 onion, halved, then quartered and sliced

1 carrot, halved lengthways, then quartered and sliced

2 garlic cloves, sliced

200 g canned chopped tomatoes

250 ml dry white wine

1 fresh bay leaf

50 g canned anchovy fillets, about 8, chopped

a handful of flat leaf parsley, chopped

coarse sea salt and freshly ground pepper

Serves 4–6

Remove any tough outer stalks from the celery and trim the tips so they will just fit into a large sauté pan with a lid.

Bring a large saucepan of water to the boil. Add a pinch of salt, then the celery and simmer gently for 10 minutes to blanch. Remove, drain and pat dry with kitchen paper.

Heat the oil in the sauté pan. Add the bacon lardons, onion and carrot and cook gently until lightly browned. Add the celery and a little salt and pepper and cook just to brown, then remove.

Add the garlic, cook for 1 minute, then add the tomatoes, wine and bay leaf. Bring to the boil and cook for 1 minute. Add the celery, cover and simmer gently for 30 minutes, turning the celery once during cooking.

Transfer the celery to a serving dish. Raise the heat and cook the sauce to reduce it slightly, about 10 minutes. Pour it over the celery, sprinkle with the anchovies and parsley and serve.

Fresh peas with lettuce form one of the classics of French cuisine. Teamed with asparagus in a light buttery sauce, they're ideal for serving with roast poultry or grilled fish. Bacon makes a nice addition and you can also stir in about 75 g fried bacon lardons, just before serving. If chervil is unavailable, use finely chopped flat leaf parsley.

peas, asparagus and baby lettuce

petits pois, asperges et laitues à la française

75 g unsalted butter

3–4 small shallots, sliced into rounds

3 Little Gem lettuces, quartered

100 g asparagus tips, halved

400 g shelled fresh peas

coarse sea salt

sprigs of chervil or scissor-snipped chives, to serve

Serves 4

Melt half the butter in a saucepan with a lid. Add the shallots and lettuce and cook, covered, stirring often, until tender, 8–10 minutes.

Season with salt, add the remaining butter and asparagus and cook for 5 minutes.

Add the peas, cover and cook for 3 more minutes. Taste for seasoning, sprinkle with the herbs and serve.

Variation For a more substantial side dish, or even a light meal, add 300 g sliced baby carrots and a splash of water when cooking the lettuce. Before serving, gently stir in more butter or 1 tablespoon crème fraîche and add 500 g boiled small new potatoes, sliced into wedges. Be sure to cook the potatoes in salted water or they will be bland.

Though pumpkin is not usually associated with French cooking, it is in fact a traditional ingredient. In the south of France, when it is in season, it often appears on menus as a gratin. The conventional recipe is simply a purée with béchamel and a topping of crisp, browned breadcrumbs. This version has rice, which gives it a more interesting texture and makes it substantial enough to be a meal on its own, served with a green salad.

pumpkin and rice gratin
gratin de courge et de riz

1.5 kg pumpkin

3 tablespoons extra virgin olive oil

100 g long grain rice

a sprig of thyme

3 tablespoons fresh breadcrumbs

a small handful of flat leaf parsley, finely chopped

3 tablespoons crème fraîche

75 g finely grated Gruyère cheese

coarse sea salt and freshly ground black pepper

a large baking dish, greased with unsalted butter

Serves 6 as a main course, 8 as a side dish

Peel and deseed the pumpkin and cut into small cubes. Put in a large saucepan with 2 tablespoons of the oil, a pinch of salt and 250 ml water. Cook over low heat, stirring often and adding more water as necessary, until soft, about 20–30 minutes.

Meanwhile, put the rice and the remaining 1 tablespoon oil in another saucepan and cook over medium heat, stirring to coat the grains. Add 250 ml water, a pinch of salt and thyme and bring to the boil. Cover and simmer until almost tender, about 10 minutes, then drain and discard the thyme.

Mix the breadcrumbs with the parsley and a pinch of salt.

Squash the cooked pumpkin into a coarse purée with a wooden spoon and stir in the rice and crème fraîche. Taste; the topping and cheese will add flavour, but the pumpkin should be seasoned as well.

Spoon the pumpkin mixture into the prepared baking dish, spreading evenly. Sprinkle the cheese in a thin layer over the top, then follow with a layer of the breadcrumbs. Bake in a preheated oven at 200°C (400°F) Gas 6 until browned, about 20–30 minutes. Serve hot.

Cream and potatoes, mingling in the heat of the oven, are almost all you'll find in this well-loved dish. If it had cheese, it wouldn't be a true dauphinois. Serve on its own, with a mixed green salad, or as a partner for simple roast meat or poultry.

creamy potato gratin
gratin dauphinois

2 kg waxy salad-style potatoes, cut into half if large

2 litres whole milk

1 fresh bay leaf

30 g unsalted butter

550 ml whipping cream

a pinch of grated nutmeg

coarse sea salt

a baking dish, 30 cm long

Serves 4–6

Put the potatoes in a large saucepan with the milk and bay leaf. Bring to the boil, then lower the heat, add a pinch of salt and simmer gently until part-cooked, 5–10 minutes.

Drain the potatoes. When cool enough to handle (but still hot), slice into rounds about 3 mm thick.

Spread the butter in the bottom of the baking dish. Arrange half the potato slices in the dish and sprinkle with salt. Put the remaining potato on top and sprinkle with more salt. Pour in the cream and sprinkle with the grated nutmeg.

Bake in a preheated oven at 180°C (350°F) Gas 4 until golden and the cream is almost absorbed, but not completely, 45 minutes. Serve hot.

A meal in itself, this is very rich and filling, just the sort of thing to serve after a day on the slopes. You might find this on menus in the Savoie region of France, though it is not, strictly speaking, a traditional recipe. It was 'invented' in the 1980s by the local cheese committee to help sell more Reblochon cheese – and I'm sold! Serve with the mixed green salad on page 25 and a bottle of chilled *vin d'Aprémont* from the Savoie, which is what you should use in the cooking.

potatoes with reblochon
tartiflette

1 kg waxy salad-style potatoes

1 fresh bay leaf

60 g unsalted butter

2 onions, halved and sliced

150 g bacon lardons

75 ml dry white wine

1 Reblochon cheese, 500 g*

coarse sea salt and freshly ground black pepper

a baking dish, about 30 cm long, greased with butter

Serves 6

Put the potatoes in a large saucepan, then add the bay leaf and cold water to cover. Bring to the boil, add a handful of salt and cook until the potatoes are *al dente*, about 15 minutes. Drain. When cool enough to handle, peel and slice.

Melt half the butter in sauté pan, add the onions and bacon lardons and cook until just browned. Remove with a slotted spoon and reserve. Add the remaining butter and the potatoes and cook gently for 5 minutes. Stir carefully without breaking too many potato slices. Add the wine, bring to the boil and boil for 1 minute. Season with salt and pepper.

Arrange the potatoes in the prepared baking dish. Scrub the rind of the cheese lightly with a vegetable brush, then cut into 8 wedges. Cut each piece in half through the middle, so each has skin on one side only. Put the cheese on top of the potatoes, skin side up. Cover with foil and bake in a preheated oven at 220°C (425°F) Gas 7 for 15 minutes. Remove the foil and bake 15–20 minutes more, until browned. Serve hot.

***Note** If Reblochon is unavailable, substitute any other French mountain cheese, such as Emmental, Cantal or a Pyrénées. Firm goats' cheese such as Crottin de Chavignol, is also very nice. Alternatively, this recipe is a great way to clear out a cluttered cheese compartment, especially the post-dinner party syndrome of lovely but unfinished cheeses. Simply crumble or slice whatever you've got and put it on top of the potatoes before baking. It will no longer be *tartiflette*, but still very much in keeping with the bistro spirit of recycling leftovers.

Thyme is omnipresent in French cuisine. Here, it transforms what would otherwise be ordinary boiled carrots into something subtly sumptuous. The crème fraîche helps too. You can substitute steamed baby leeks for the carrots, but stir in a tablespoon or so of butter when adding the crème fraîche.

carrots with cream and herbs
carottes à la crème aux herbes

800 g mini carrots, trimmed, or medium carrots

50 g unsalted butter

a sprig of thyme

2 tablespoons crème fraîche

several sprigs of chervil

a small bunch of chives

fine sea salt

Serves 4

If using larger carrots, cut them diagonally into 5 cm slices. Put in a large saucepan (the carrots should fit in almost a single layer for even cooking). Add the butter and set over low heat. Cook to melt and coat, about 3 minutes. Half fill the saucepan with water, then add a pinch of salt and the thyme. Cover and cook until the water is almost completely evaporated, 10–20 minutes.

Stir in the cream and add salt to taste. Using kitchen scissors, snip the chervil and chives over the top, mix well and serve.

Variation In spring, when turnips are sweet, they make a nice addition to this dish. Peel and quarter large turnips, or just peel baby ones – the main thing is to ensure that all the vegetable pieces (carrot and turnip) are about the same size so that they cook evenly. Halve the carrot quantity and complete with turnips, or double the recipe. Sprinkle with a large handful of just-cooked shelled peas before serving for extra crunch and pretty colour.

French beans are the classic accompaniment for lamb, but they are equally nice with fish and chicken. You can also serve at room temperature, as part of a salad buffet. Instead of the cooked beans, try long, thin slices of steamed courgettes, sautéed with the garlic.

french beans with garlic
haricots verts à l'ail

625 g small green beans, trimmed

2 tablespoons extra virgin olive oil

1 tablespoon unsalted butter

2 garlic cloves, crushed

a handful of flat leaf parsley, chopped

1 teaspoon freshly squeezed lemon juice (optional)

coarse sea salt and freshly ground black pepper

Serves 4

Bring a large saucepan of water to the boil. Add the beans and cook for 3–4 minutes from the time the water returns to the boil. Drain and refresh under cold running water. Set aside.

Heat the oil and butter in a frying pan. Add the garlic, beans and salt, and cook on high for 1 minute, stirring. Remove from the heat and stir in the parsley and lemon juice, if using. Sprinkle with pepper and serve.

Variation Flageolet beans are the other traditional partner for lamb. Generally, dried beans taste better if cooked from scratch, but this does require advance planning. Happily, I find that flageolets are the exception, especially if you can find imported French flageolets in jars, not cans. For mixed beans to serve with lamb (for four), halve the quantity of green beans and add a 400 g jar of drained beans to the cooked green beans when frying with the garlic. Instead of lemon juice, stir in 3–4 tablespoons crème fraîche just before serving.

A regular accompaniment on the *plat du jour* circuit, this recipe goes especially well with pork. The secret of delicious cauliflower is to blanch it first; if you parboil it with a bay leaf, the unpleasant cabbage aroma disappears.

cauliflower gratin
gratin de chou-fleur

1 large cauliflower, separated into large florets

1 fresh bay leaf

500 ml double cream

1 egg, beaten

2 teaspoons Dijon mustard

160 g finely grated Comté cheese*

coarse sea salt

a baking dish, about 25 cm diameter, greased with butter

Serves 4–6

Bring a large saucepan of water to the boil, add the bay leaf, salt generously, then add the cauliflower. Cook until still slightly firm, about 10 minutes. Drain and set aside.

Put the cream in a saucepan and bring to the boil. Boil for 10 minutes. Add a spoonful of hot milk to the beaten egg to warm it, then stir in the egg, mustard and 1 teaspoon salt.

Divide the cauliflower into smaller florets, then stir into the cream sauce. Transfer to the prepared dish and sprinkle the cheese over the top in an even layer. Bake in a preheated oven at 200°C (400°F) Gas 6 until golden, about 40–45 minutes. Serve hot.

*Note Like Gruyère, Comté is a mountain cheese – from the Franche-Comté region to be precise – but the similarity stops there. Comté's distinct flavour comes from the milk used in the making, so the flavour varies with the seasons. A springtime diet of tender young shoots delivers milk that is very different from its winter counterpart, nourished mainly on hay. I've never met a Comté I didn't like, but it is darker in colour and fruitier in summer, paler and more nutty in winter. Use Emmental or Cantal if it is unavailable, or see page 142 for French cheese websites.

Tian is the Provençal name for a square earthenware dish, but I use a non-stick roasting tin and the tian still tastes great. Ideally, it should be served tepid or at room temperature, as it would be for the sweltering heat of a Provençal summer. The tian will improve with age and can easily be made one day in advance.

4 medium aubergines, sliced crossways into 2 cm pieces

5 tablespoons fresh breadcrumbs

½ teaspoon herbes de provence

about 125 ml extra virgin olive oil

2 large onions, sliced into thick rings

3 large tomatoes, sliced (not beefsteak)

40 g pitted black olives, sliced

coarse sea salt and freshly ground black pepper

Tomato sauce

1 tablespoon extra virgin olive oil

3 garlic cloves

1.5 kg tomatoes, skinned, deseeded and chopped

a pinch of sugar

a small handful of basil, chopped

a small handful of flat leaf parsley, chopped

coarse sea salt and freshly ground black pepper

non-stick roasting tin or earthenware dish

Serves 4–6

aubergine, onion and tomato tian

tian d'aubergines aux oignons et tomates

To make the tomato sauce, heat the oil in a saucepan, add the garlic and cook until just soft, 1–2 minutes. Add the tomatoes, sugar, and salt to taste. Cover and simmer gently for 10 minutes. Stir in the basil and parsley and set aside.

Bring a large saucepan of water to the boil and add a pinch of salt. Add the aubergine slices and cook until just blanched and tender, 3–5 minutes. Drain well.

Put the breadcrumbs, herbs and a pinch of salt in a bowl, stir well and set aside.

Pour 3–4 tablespoons of the oil in the baking dish, arrange the aubergine rounds on top and drizzle with some of the remaining oil. Top with the onion rings and sprinkle with salt and pepper. Dot the sauce on top, spreading as evenly as possible. Arrange the tomato slices on top, sprinkle with the breadcrumbs, followed by the olives. Bake in a preheated oven at 200°C (400°F) Gas 6 until well browned, about 45 minutes. Serve hot or warm.

I first learned to make ratatouille from a friend's mother in her kitchen in Aix-en-Provence. Her method involves adding each vegetable separately, in the order which best suits their cooking requirements. It does make a difference because I've rarely tasted a ratatouille as good. It is also important to season each vegetable 'layer' individually. Finally, I prefer my ratatouille vegetables to be distinct from each another, so cut the pieces medium-large, about 3–4 cm. Serve with crusty bread.

ratatouille

1 kg aubergines, cut into pieces

extra virgin olive oil (see method)

2 medium onions, coarsely chopped

2 red peppers, halved, deseeded and cut into pieces

2 yellow peppers, halved, deseeded and cut into pieces

1 green pepper, halved, deseeded and cut into pieces

6 smallish courgettes, about 750 g, halved lengthways and sliced

4 garlic cloves, crushed

6 medium tomatoes, halved, deseeded and chopped

a small bunch of basil, coarsely chopped

coarse sea salt

To serve

a few basil leaves, finely sliced

1 garlic clove, crushed

Serves 4–6

Put the aubergine pieces in a microwave-proof bowl with 3 tablespoons water and microwave on HIGH for 6 minutes. Drain and set aside.

Heat 3 tablespoons of the oil in a large casserole with a lid. Add the onions and cook until soft, 3–5 minutes. Salt lightly.

Add all the peppers and cook for 5–8 minutes more, stirring often. Turn up the heat to keep the sizzling sound going, but take care not to let it burn. Salt lightly.

Add 1 more tablespoon of the oil and the courgettes. Mix well and cook for about 5 minutes more, stirring occasionally. Salt lightly.

Add 2 more tablespoons of the oil and the drained aubergines. Cook, stirring often, for 5 minutes more. Salt lightly.

Add the garlic and cook for 1 minute. Add 1 more tablespoon of the oil if necessary, and the tomatoes and basil and stir well. Salt lightly. Cook for 5 minutes, then cover, lower the heat and simmer gently for 30 minutes, checking occasionally.

Remove from the heat. This is best served at room temperature, but it still tastes nice hot. The longer you let it stand, the richer it tastes. Stir in extra basil and garlic just before serving.

There are several regional variations on this recipe and it was difficult to choose which one to include. *Chou rouge à la flammande* has apples, *à la limousine* has chestnuts. This has it all, with some Alsatian Riesling and bacon as well – serve it with grilled sausages, pork chops or roasts, and the same wine as used in the cooking. It is also fantastic with Christmas goose.

braised red cabbage
with chestnuts and apples
chou rouge aux marrons et aux pommes

1 red cabbage

3 tablespoons unsalted butter

1 onion, halved and thinly sliced

75 g bacon lardons

3 cooking apples, peeled, cored and chopped

200 g vacuum-packed whole peeled chestnuts

2 teaspoons coarse sea salt

250 ml dry white wine, preferably Riesling

1 tablespoon sugar

Serves 4–6

Cut the cabbage in quarters, then core and slice thinly.

Melt 2 tablespoons of the butter in a sauté pan. Add the onion and lardons and cook until soft, about 3 minutes.

Add the remaining butter, the cabbage, apples and chestnuts and stir well. Season with salt, then add the wine, sugar and 250 ml water.

Bring to the boil, boil for 1 minute, then cover and simmer gently until the cabbage is tender, about 45 minutes.

Years ago, my husband and I went on a wine-buying mission with some friends in the Jura region of France. We stopped for lunch at a small hotel, but it was very late in the day, so we had to take what we were given. The offering was roast pork, served with a glorious mixture of vegetables, all thinly sliced and baked in a fabulous savoury custard. Back home, I tried a similar dish using just spinach, because that's what was on hand, and it proved a great success.

spinach flan
flan d'épinards

500 g fresh spinach
3–5 tablespoons extra virgin olive oil
200 ml crème fraîche
2 eggs
1 teaspoon coarse sea salt
a pinch of freshly grated nutmeg
1 tablespoon unsalted butter

a baking dish, 30 cm long

Serves 4

Wash the spinach, then spin-dry in a salad spinner. Working in batches, heat 1 tablespoon of the oil in a non-stick frying pan and add a mound of spinach. Cook the spinach over high heat, stirring until all the leaves have just wilted. Transfer to a plastic colander and let drain. Continue cooking until all the spinach has been wilted.

Chop the spinach coarsely. Put the crème fraîche, eggs, salt and nutmeg in a bowl and whisk well. Stir in the spinach.

Spread the butter in the bottom of a baking dish. Transfer the spinach mixture to the dish and bake in a preheated oven at 180°C (350°F) Gas 4 until just set, 25–30 minutes. Serve hot.

This bistro classic is a much more sophisticated version of macaroni and cheese. It is ideal for serving with beef stews, as the gratin is even better when mixed with broth.

macaroni gratin
gratin de macaroni

300 g thin macaroni

500 ml milk

3 tablespoons crème fraîche

60 g unsalted butter

4 tablespoons plain flour

coarse sea salt and freshly ground black pepper

200 g finely grated Beaufort cheese*

a baking dish, 30 cm long, greased with butter

Serves 6

Cook the macaroni in plenty of boiling, well-salted water according to the instructions on the packet. Drain, rinse well and return to the empty saucepan.

Heat the milk in a saucepan and stir in the crème fraîche. Melt the butter in a second saucepan over medium-high heat. Stir in the flour and cook, stirring constantly for 3 minutes. Pour in the milk mixture and stir constantly until the mixture thickens. Season with salt and pepper.

Stir the milk mixture into the macaroni and taste, adding salt and pepper if necessary. Transfer to the baking dish and sprinkle with the cheese. Cook under a preheated grill until bubbling and browned, 10–15 minutes. Serve hot.

*Note Beaufort is an alpine cheese, similar to Gruyère, but with a slightly sweeter, more pronounced nutty flavour. It is becoming more widely available outside France, my local supermarket always has some, but if you cannot find it, Emmental, Cantal or any firm, Cheddar-like cheese will do. The taste will be entirely different, of course.

sweet things

As soon as it's strawberry season, you'll find this on menus all over France, though Plougastel in Brittany claims to be home to the best of the French strawberry crop. Wherever they come from, lemon juice is key, enhancing the flavour of the fruit as well as adding tartness to show off the sugar. Be sure to taste before adding all the lemon juice; the amount can vary depending on the quality of the strawberries. This is as much blueprint as recipe so, once you've made it the traditional way, try it other ways. Use clementine, orange or lime juice instead of lemon and sprinkle with a small handful of chopped fresh mint leaves, for example. You can also serve it with slices of Madeira cake or rolled into crêpes, and pass the whipped cream or vanilla ice cream.

sugared strawberries
fraises au sucre

1 kg strawberries, at room temperature
freshly squeezed juice of 1 lemon
3–5 tablespoons caster sugar
crème fraîche or whipped cream, to serve

Serves 4–6

Trim the strawberries and put in a pretty bowl. Add the lemon juice and 3 tablespoons of the sugar. Mix gently but thoroughly and let stand about 15 minutes. Taste, and add more sugar if necessary.

This dish improves with standing, but don't leave it too long. If you make it just before you're ready to begin your meal, it will be ready in time for pudding.

If using crème fraîche, sweeten it with a spoonful of caster sugar.

Variation Peach or nectarine slices can be substituted for the strawberries, if you like to stick to single fruit, or use a mixture of soft fruit including redcurrants, blueberries, raspberries and blackberries.

These are neither too sweet, nor too heavy; the perfect ending to a substantial bistro-style meal. Preparation is simple but there are a few tricks to facilitate unmoulding. First, don't use moulds that are too deep (and don't overfill them). Then, let the custards stand in the bain-marie for a good 15 minutes before removing them to cool completely. According to a reliable old French cookbook of mine, this allows the custard to settle and solidify, making it easier to turn out. Just before serving, run a knife around the inside edge, hold an upturned plate over the top and flip over to release the custard.

caramel custard
crème renversée au caramel

750 ml whole milk

1 vanilla pod, split lengthways with a small sharp knife

180 g sugar

5 eggs

a pinch of salt

8 ramekin dishes

a roasting tin to hold the ramekins

Serves 8

Put the milk, vanilla pod and its seeds in a saucepan and bring to the boil over medium heat. Immediately remove from the heat, cover and let stand while you make the caramel.

To make the caramel, put 100 g of the sugar, the salt and 4 tablespoons water in a small heavy-based saucepan, preferably with a pouring lip. Heat until the sugar turns a deep caramel colour, then remove from the heat. When it stops sizzling, pour carefully into the ramekins. Take care not to let the caramel come into contact with your skin; it is very hot. Set the ramekins in a roasting tin and add enough boiling water to come half-way up the sides – this is called a bain-marie. Set aside.

Add the remaining 80 g sugar and the salt to the saucepan of warm milk and stir until dissolved. Remove the vanilla pod.

Crack the eggs into another bowl and whisk until smooth. Pour the warm milk into the eggs and stir well. Ladle into the ramekins.

Carefully transfer the bain-marie with the ramekins into a preheated oven at 180°C (350°F) Gas 4 and bake until the custard is set and a knife inserted into the middle comes out clean, about 20–25 minutes. Serve at room temperature either in their ramekins or inverted onto a plate so the caramel forms a pool of sweet sauce.

This is very easy to make and ideal for entertaining, since it should be made one day in advance. It is also deceptively rich, thanks to the egg yolks, which can be reduced in quantity or omitted altogether. It is important to use good-quality chocolate, but anything over 70 per cent cocoa solids will be too much. In traditional bistros, chocolate mousse is often served in a single, large bowl and passed around the table for diners to help themselves, so if you're expecting a crowd, double the recipe and do the same.

chocolate mousse

mousse au chocolat

200 g dark chocolate, broken into pieces

30 g unsalted butter, cut into small pieces

1 vanilla pod, split lengthways with a small sharp knife

3 eggs, separated

a pinch of salt

2 tablespoons caster sugar

sweetened crème fraîche or whipped cream, to serve (optional)

Serves 4

Put the chocolate in a glass bowl and melt in the microwave on HIGH for 40 seconds. Remove, stir and repeat until almost completely melted. Remove, then stir in the butter. Using the tip of a small knife, scrape the small black seeds from the vanilla pod into the chocolate. Add the egg yolks, stir and set aside.

Using an electric mixer, beat the egg whites and salt until foaming. Continue beating and add the sugar. Beat on high until glossy and firm.

Carefully fold the whites into the chocolate with a rubber spatula until no more white specks can be seen.

Transfer the mousse to serving dishes and refrigerate for at least 6 hours, but overnight is best.

This is a very simple, classic recipe and there are hundreds of versions. Some cook on top of the stove, some call for long grain rice, some add eggs or egg yolks and some add flavourings such as orange peel or cinnamon. One thing that is fairly consistent among French recipes is the double rice-cooking method and the reason is that blanching the rice first removes much of the starch. The result is light and delicate, not blobby and glutinous like some puddings I've tasted. The list of things to serve with it is fairly unlimited. Cooked and puréed apples or apricots, red fruit coulis, chocolate sauce and custard sauce are traditional, but the American in me likes cranberry sauce. Of course, it's also very nice just as it is.

rice pudding
riz au lait

125 g risotto rice, such as arborio

500 ml whole milk, boiled

60 g sugar

1 vanilla pod, split lengthways with a small sharp knife

15 g unsalted butter

a pinch of salt

Serves 4

Put the rice in a saucepan with a lid and add cold water to cover. Slowly bring to the boil over medium heat, then boil for 5 minutes. Drain the rice and rinse under cold water. Set aside to drain well.

Meanwhile, put the milk in an ovenproof pan with a lid and bring to the boil. Add the sugar and vanilla pod. Remove from the heat, cover and let stand for 15 minutes. Using the tip of the knife, scrape out the vanilla seeds and stir them through the milk.

Add the rice to the milk, then add the butter and salt. Bring slowly to the boil. Cover and transfer to a preheated oven at 180°C (350°F) Gas 4. Do not stir. Cook until the rice is tender and the liquid is almost completely absorbed but not dry, about 25–35 minutes. Serve warm.

In summer, many bistro menus feature clafoutis, a custard-like batter baked with whole cherries – a speciality of the Limousin region. It is one of the finest French puddings, and a cinch to make. The only drawback is that the cherry season is a short one, and it is a shame to limit clafoutis making to just one part of the year. Plums, pears and apples work well as substitutes, but rhubarb is fantastic. Almost better than the original, I think.

rhubarb clafoutis
clafoutis à la rhubarbe

500 g fresh rhubarb, cut into 3 cm slices

200 ml whole milk

200 ml double cream

3 eggs

150 g sugar

¼ teaspoon ground cinnamon

a pinch of salt

1 vanilla pod, split lengthways with a small sharp knife

50 g plain flour

a large baking dish, about 30 cm diameter, greased with butter and sprinkled with sugar

Serves 6

Bring a saucepan of water to the boil, add the rhubarb and cook for 2 minutes, just to blanch. Drain and set aside.

Put the milk, cream, eggs, sugar, cinnamon and salt in a bowl and mix well. Using the tip of a knife, scrape the vanilla seeds into the mixture. Add the flour and whisk well.

Arrange the rhubarb pieces in the prepared dish. Pour the batter over the top and bake in a preheated oven at 200°C (400°F) Gas 6 until puffed and golden, about 40–45 minutes.

Golden Delicious is the apple of preference for most French dishes. It's not an especially interesting eating variety, but it's perfect for baking and cooking. It holds its shape well and is not too tart. The vanilla-scented purée is an extra, but worth the indulgence.

simple apple tart
tarte aux pommes

200 g plain flour,
plus extra for rolling

2 teaspoons caster sugar

100 g cold unsalted butter,
cut into pieces

a pinch of salt

Apple purée

3 Golden Delicious apples,
peeled and chopped

1 vanilla pod, split lengthways
with a small sharp knife

2 tablespoons sugar

10 g unsalted butter

Apple topping

3 Golden Delicious apples,
peeled and sliced

15 g unsalted butter, melted

1 tablespoon sugar

*baking parchment and beans or
baking weights*

*a loose-based tart tin,
27 cm diameter, greased and floured*

Serves 6

To make the pastry, put the flour, sugar, butter and salt in a food processor and, using the pulse button, process until the butter is broken down (5–10 pulses). Add 3 tablespoons cold water and pulse just until the dough forms coarse crumbs; add 1 more tablespoon if necessary, but do not do more than 10 pulses.

Transfer the pastry to a sheet of baking parchment, form into a ball and flatten to a disc. Wrap in the parchment and refrigerate for 30–60 minutes.

Roll out the pastry on a floured work surface to a disc slightly larger than the tart tin. Carefully transfer the pastry to the tin, patching any holes as you go and pressing gently into the sides. To trim the edges, roll a rolling pin over the top, using the edge of the tin as a cutting surface, and letting the excess fall away. Tidy up the edges and refrigerate until firm, about 30–60 minutes.

Prick the pastry all over, line with the parchment paper and fill with beans or baking weights. Bake in a preheated oven at 200°C (400°F) Gas 6 for 15 minutes, then remove the paper and weights and bake until just golden, 10–15 minutes more. Let the tart shell cool slightly before filling.

To make the apple purée, put the chopped apples, vanilla pod, sugar and butter in a saucepan, add 4 tablespoons water and cook gently, stirring often until soft, adding more water if necessary, about 10–15 minutes. Use the tip of a small knife to scrape the seeds out of the vanilla pod into the purée, then discard the pod. Transfer the mixture to a food processor, blender or food mill and purée.

Spread the purée evenly in the tart shell. Arrange the apple slices in a circle around the edge; they should be slightly overlapping but not completely squashed together. Repeat for an inner circle, trimming the slices slightly so they fit, and going in the opposite direction from the outer circle. Brush with the melted butter and sprinkle with the sugar. Bake in a preheated oven at 200°C (400°F) Gas 6 until just browned and tender, about 25–35 minutes. Serve warm or at room temperature.

This is elegant, both in appearance and flavour. It is ideal for entertaining since the tart shell and almond cream can be made a few hours in advance. To make it even more special, serve with crème fraîche sweetened with some caster sugar, or good quality vanilla ice cream.

pear and almond tart
tarte aux poires frangipane

200 g plain flour, plus extra for rolling

2 teaspoons caster sugar

100 g cold unsalted butter, cut into pieces

a pinch of salt

3–4 ripe pears*

Almond cream

100 g butter

100 g sugar

2 eggs

100 ground almonds

2 tablespoons flour

baking parchment and beans or baking weights

a loose-based tart tin, 27 cm diameter, greased and floured

Serves 6

*If only unripe pears are available, poach them for 5 minutes in a saucepan of water with the freshly squeezed juice of ½ lemon

To make the pastry, put the flour, sugar, butter and salt in a food processor and, using the pulse button, process until the butter is broken down (about 5–10 pulses). Add 3 tablespoons cold water and pulse until the mixture forms coarse crumbs; add 1 more tablespoon if necessary but do not do more than 10 pulses.

Transfer the pastry to a sheet of baking parchment, form into a ball and flatten to a disc. Wrap in paper and let stand for 30–60 minutes.

Roll out the pastry on a floured work surface to a disc slightly larger than the tart tin. Carefully transfer the pastry to the tin, patching any holes as you go and pressing gently into the sides. To trim the edges, roll a rolling pin over the top, using the edge of the tin as a cutting surface, and letting the excess fall away. Tidy up the edges and refrigerate until firm, about 30–60 minutes.

Prick the pastry all over, line with the baking parchment and fill with beans or baking weights. Bake on a low shelf in a preheated oven at 200°C (400°F) Gas 6 for 15 minutes, then remove the paper and weights and bake until just golden, 10–15 minutes more. Let the tart shell cool slightly before filling.

Meanwhile, to make the almond cream, put the butter and sugar in a bowl and beat with an electric mixer until fluffy and lemon-coloured. Beat in the eggs, one at a time. Using a spatula, fold in the almonds and flour until well mixed.

Lower the oven temperature to 190°C (375°F) Gas 5. Spread the almond cream evenly in the tart shell.

Peel and slice the pears, into 8 or 12 slices, depending on the size of the pears. Arrange the pear slices on top of the almond cream.

Bake until puffed and golden, about 20–25 minutes. Serve warm.

When my son was little, we spent two weeks every September in a small village near Bandol, on the Mediterranean. The Sunday morning market was fantastic, but my favourite stall was held by a local farm woman, who sold fresh eggs, tree-ripened fruit, herbs and jars of the most delicious homemade jams I've ever tasted. The best was peach and redcurrant, a match made in heaven, so I've adapted a classic apple tart recipe in her honour. Sometimes she used white peaches, and you should too, if they're available.

peach and redcurrant tart
tarte aux pêches et aux groseilles

200 g plain flour, plus extra for rolling

2 teaspoons caster sugar

100 g cold unsalted butter, cut into pieces

a pinch of salt

3–4 tablespoons cold water

Peach and redcurrant filling

3 eggs

3 tablespoons crème fraîche

50 g sugar

3 large ripe peaches, thinly sliced

4–5 stems of redcurrants, about 50 g

a loose-based tart tin, 27 cm diameter, greased and floured

baking parchment and baking beans or weights

Serves 12

To make the pastry, put the flour, sugar, butter and salt in a food processor and, using the pulse button, process until the butter is broken down (about 5–10 pulses). Add 3 tablespoons of the cold water and pulse just until the dough forms coarse crumbs; add 1 more tablespoon if necessary, but don't do more than 10 pulses.

Transfer the pastry to a sheet of baking parchment, form into a ball and flatten to a disc. Wrap in the parchment and let stand for 30–60 minutes.

Roll out the pastry on a floured work surface to a disc slightly larger than the tart tin. Carefully transfer the pastry to the prepared tin, patching any holes as you go and pressing gently into the sides. To trim the edges, roll a rolling pin over the top, using the edge of the tin as a cutting surface, and letting the excess fall away. Tidy up the edges and refrigerate until firm, 30–60 minutes.

Preheat the oven to 200°C (400°F) Gas 6. Prick the pastry all over, line with baking parchment and fill with baking beans or weights. Bake for 15 minutes, then remove the paper and weights and bake until just golden, 10–15 minutes more. Let the tart shell cool slightly before filling.

To make the filling, put the eggs, crème fraîche and sugar in a bowl and whisk well. Arrange the peach slices in 2 circles inside the cooled tart shell. The inner circle should go in the opposite direction from the outer circle. Pour in the egg mixture and sprinkle the redcurrants on top.

Bake until puffed and just beginning to brown, 25–30 minutes. Serve warm or at room temperature.

Any bistro worthy of the name will have a chocolate cake on its menu. This one is special because of the hazelnuts – a grown-up version of Nutella. Unusually, this recipe works best with ordinary plain chocolate with no more than 50 per cent cocoa solids.

chocolate-hazelnut cake
gâteau au chocolat et aux noisettes

100 g shelled hazelnuts

150 g dark chocolate, broken into pieces

75 g unsalted butter

125 g caster sugar

4 eggs, separated

100 g plain flour

a pinch of salt

4 tablespoons crème fraîche

double cream or crème fraîche, sweetened, to serve

To decorate

50 g chocolate

1 tablespoon icing sugar

1 tablespoon cocoa powder

a cake tin, 23 cm diameter, greased

Serves 8

Put 80 g of the hazelnuts in a small food processor and grind to a powder. Set aside.

Put the chocolate and butter in a glass bowl and microwave on HIGH for about 1½ minutes until almost completely melted. Stir, then let stand until fully melted.

Reserve 1 tablespoon of sugar and put the remainder in a large bowl. Add the egg yolks, then beat until fluffy and lemon-coloured. Stir in the chocolate mixture, then the flour, salt, hazelnuts and crème fraîche. The mixture will be slightly stiff.

Put the egg whites in another bowl and beat with an electric hand mixer until frothy. Add the reserved 1 tablespoon sugar and beat on high until they hold stiff peaks. Using a rubber spatula, fold one-third of the egg whites into the chocolate mixture. Add the remaining whites, folding just until there are no more specks of white.

Transfer to the prepared cake tin and bake in a preheated oven at 180°C (350°F) Gas 4 until a knife inserted in the middle comes out clean, about 20–30 minutes. Let cool slightly, then turn out onto a wire rack to cool.

To decorate, toast the remaining 20 g hazelnuts in a dry frying pan and crush lightly. Microwave the chocolate on HIGH for 30 seconds, then shave off curls with a vegetable peeler. Set aside. Put the icing sugar and cocoa in a sieve and hold it over the cake. Tap the edge of the sieve to release the mixture, moving around the cake to coat. A very light dusting is sufficient. Sprinkle the chocolate and toasted hazelnuts in the centre. Serve at room temperature, with lots of sweetened whipped cream or crème fraîche. The cake will keep well for several days in an airtight container.

Strictly speaking, this is more home cooking than bistro, but the line is a fine one and this recipe is too good not to include. The yoghurt pot is the measure, so it doesn't really matter what size – or flavour – you use, but plain, French-style set yoghurt is my preference. If you don't fancy orange, try other flavourings: cinnamon, honey, vanilla, chocolate, fruit pieces ... This is great to make, and eat, with children.

yoghurt cake
gâteau au yaourt

125 g plain set yoghurt

2 pots sugar

3 pots flour

2 eggs

1 tablespoon sunflower oil

1 teaspoon bicarbonate of soda

a pinch of salt

freshly squeezed juice of 1 orange

1 tablespoon icing sugar, to decorate

a deep cake tin, 23 cm diameter, greased

Serves 8

Empty the yoghurt into a large bowl and wipe out the pot so when you measure the other ingredients, they won't stick. Add the sugar, flour, eggs, oil, bicarbonate of soda, salt and half the orange juice. Stir well.

Pour into the prepared cake tin and bake in a preheated oven at 180°C (350°F) Gas 4 until a knife inserted in the middle comes out clean, about 15–20 minutes. Remove from the oven and pierce a few holes in the top with a fork. Pour over the remaining orange juice. Let cool slightly, then turn out onto a wire rack to cool.

To decorate, put the icing sugar in a sieve and hold it over the cake. Tap the edge of the sieve to release the sugar, moving around the surface to coat. A very light dusting is sufficient. Serve at room temperature.

mail order and websites

POULTRY AND MEAT

Cornvale Foods
Station Yard, Melling, Kirkby, Lonsdale
Carnforth, Lancashire LA6 2QY
Tel: 015242 22420
Fax: 015242 22350
Email: queries@cornvalefoods.co.uk
www.cornvalefoods.co.uk
*Friendly and helpful, able to supply
guinea fowl, rabbit and other meats.*

The Country Butcher
Tel: 01452 831585
www.countrybutcher.co.uk
*Award-winning sausages, traditional
bacon.*

Ellel Free Range Poultry Company
The Stables, Ellel Grange, Galgate
Nr Lancaster, Lancashire LA2 0HN
Tel: 01524 751200
Fax: 01524 752648
www.ellelfreerangepoultry.co.uk
For good-quality guinea fowl.

Providence Farm Organic Meats
Tel: 01409 254421
www.providencefarm.co.uk
Organic pork, beef, chicken and duck.

The Real Meat Company
Warminster BA12 0HR
Tel: 01985 840562
Fax: 01985 841005
Email: richard@realmeat.co.uk
*For listing of butchers nationwide
who stock Real Meat Company
products, also online buying. Good
source for rabbit.*

Scottish Organic Meats
Tel: 01899 221747
www.scottishorganicmeats.com
Organic beef, lamb, pork, chicken.

Simply Sausages
Unit 13, Bermondsey Trading Estate
Rotherhithe New Road
London SE16 3LL
Tel: 020 7394 7776
Fax: 020 7394 9477
www.simplysa.dircon.co.uk
*Makers of lovely sausages, especially
authentic Toulouse for cassoulet.*

FISH

The Fish Society
Tel: 0800 074 6859
www.thefishsociety.co.uk
*Fresh fish including organic and wild
salmon, smoked fish and shellfish.
Next day delivery.*

Seafooddirect
Tel: 08000 851549
www.seafooddirect.co.uk
Home delivery of fish and seafood.

Wing of St Mawes
Tel: 0800 052 3717
www.cornish-seafood.co.uk
*Fresh and smoked fish. Next day
delivery.*

GENERAL FOOD

The Fresh Food Company
Tel: 020 8749 8778
www.freshfood.co.uk
*Weekly box delivery nationwide: meat
(including rabbit), fish, vegetables, fruit,
bread, wine and beer.*

Soil Association
Bristol House, 40–56 Victoria Street,
Bristol, BS1 6BY
Tel: 0117 929 0661
Fax: 0117 925 2504
Email: info@soilassociation.org
www.soilassociation.org.uk
*Listing of organic meat, vegetable and
other quality UK foodstuff suppliers.*

Selfridges Food Hall
Selfridges, 400 Oxford Street,
London W1A 1AB
Tel: 0870 8377377
*Good for duck and goose confit. Mail
order available.*

KITCHEN EQUIPMENT

The Cooks Kitchen
Tel: 0117 9070903 for catalogue.
Online mail order:
www.kitchenware.co.uk
*Mail order company with everything
you could need for pastry-making and
baking, including rolling pins, ceramic
baking beans, best-quality heavy duty
tins and baking sheets and more.*

Divertimenti
139–141 Fulham Road
London SW3 6SD
Tel: 020 7581 8065
Fax: 020 7823 9429
33–34 Marylebone High Street
London W1U 4PT
Tel: 020 7935 0689
www.divertimenti.co.uk
*Two London shops plus mail order for
a wide range of equipment. Knife
sharpening and copper retinning service.*

Leon Jaeggi & Sons
77 Shaftesbury Avenue
London W1V 7DJ
Tel: 020 7434 4545
*Professional catering equipment, open
to the public.*

Lakeland Limited
Alexandra Buildings, Windermere
Cumbria LA23 1BQ
Tel: 015394 88100
Fax: 015394 88300
www.lakelandlimited.com
*Huge range of high-quality bakeware
and cookery equipment available by
mail order, online and from their
shops. Some hard-to-find ingredients
also available. Phone for a catalogue.*

David Mellor
4 Sloane Square London SW1 8EE
Tel: 020 7730 4259
www.davidmellordesign.co.uk
Shop, mail order catalogue.

Nisbets
Freepost BS4675
Bristol BS2 0YZ
Tel: 0117 955583
www.nisbets.co.uk
*A comprehensive guide to light
catering equipment.*

W.M. Page
121 Shaftesbury Avenue
London WC2H 8AD
Tel: 020 7565 5959
Excellent baking equipment.

Silverwood Limited
Ledsam Street Works
Birmingham B16 8DN
Tel: 0121 454 3571/2
Fax: 0121 454 6749
Email: Sales@AlanSilverwood.co.uk
*Professional quality bread and cake
tins and trays, bakeware which should
last a lifetime, plus Aga range too.
Stocked by Lakeland, John Lewis
stores, major department stores and
cook shops. For local stockists write
or phone for details.*

Wares of Knutsford
Household and Hardware Emporium
36a Princess St, Knutsford, Cheshire
Tel: 01565 751477
Mail order at:
www.waresofknutsford.co.uk
*Good old-fashioned quality
ironmongers selling a selection of
kitchen and bakeware including tins,
measuring jugs and measuring spoons.*

SPECIALITY ITEMS

Extra Virgin Olive Oils and Mediterranean Foods
Tel: 01460 72931
www.getoily.com
*Olive oils, nut oils and Mediterranean
produce.*

French cheese
www.frencheese.co.uk
*A website devoted to the cheese of
France, with directory of stockists.*

Kanbil
Irazabala, 64250 Espelette, Pays Basque
Tel: 33 (0)5-59-93-93-02
Fax: 33 (0)5-59-93-80-18
*Mail order suppliers of piment
d'espelette, French-language site.*

WINE

Yapp Brothers
Mere, Wiltshire BA12 6DY
Tel: 01747 860423
Fax: 01747 860929
Email: sales@yapp.co.uk
www.yapp.co.uk

index